THE
ART OF WAR
PUZZLE BOOK

THE
ART OF WAR
PUZZLE BOOK

Challenges of strategy, intelligence, and surprise

ROLAND HALL

SIRIUS

SIRIUS

This edition published in 2024 by Sirius Publishing, a division of
Arcturus Publishing Limited,
26/27 Bickels Yard, 151–153 Bermondsey Street,
London SE1 3HA

ISBN: 978-1-3988-3627-3
AD011276NT

Printed in China

Contents

Introduction

When Sun Tzu wrote *The Art of War* around two thousand years ago, the military leader and master tactician could have had no idea of the impact his words would have around the world, for such a long period of time. Even more interesting is that his words have been used so extensively in contexts other than war. There are plenty of places outside of a battlefield where conflict-free resolution is optimum: business, law, education, and sports in particular, but you could apply some of the lessons in many aspects of daily life. The lessons taught are universal and timeless, and may be applied to a wide variety of situations by people from all walks of lfe.

This is reminiscent of a good puzzle. A good puzzle is a challenge to overcome; an adversary to beat; a problem to solve. These days, of course, you can look up a puzzle's solution on the Internet, and even if you do not find that particular answer you will probably find one that is close. Maybe even AI will be able to help you (I doubt it). But an answer found that way deprives you of the satisfaction of finding something yourself, of using your brainpower to overcome that obstacle—the strategic element if you will—all on your own. And strategy is what *The Art of War* is all about: preparation, awareness, and common sense. Of course—and this is no coincidence—all of those traits are useful when it comes to solving puzzles too.

All the puzzles in this book are solvable with a little thought and application. Admittedly some are a bit tougher than others, and some you may find more annoying than others when you see the simple answer before you (or work it out for yourself).

The puzzles take place with a theme of conflict at heart, whether that is an actual historical war, a boardroom tussle, a legend, or a simple argument. Each one comes with a quote from the great book, either to provide inspiration, a clue, or simply to add a little something extra to the world.

We hope you enjoy the challenges we have set you, there is something for everyone within these pages and we hope you are stimulated and rise to the challenge. And remember: "All warfare is based on deception", so make sure you read the puzzles carefully if you want to solve them successfully—things are not always as they appear to be, and many puzzles require a clear mind and a thoughtful brain…

Puzzles

Heaven or Hel

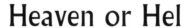

"Heaven: one of the five constant factors."

Bodil dies on the battlefield so expects to go to Valhalla with Odin. However, on his way to the realms above, he is confronted with a choice of gates and one final challenge. One leads to Valhalla, the other to Hel, the underworld where an eternity of misery awaits. Before each gate stands a gatekeeper—a fierce warrior. Bodil knows from legend that one gatekeeper always tells the truth, the other always lies. Bodil is allowed to ask one question—and one question only. What should it be? Your answer will have an effect for eternity, so make it wise.

The Jester's Riddle

*"Conceal your dispositions, and you will be safe
from the prying of the subtlest spies."*

"Come, come, my brave knights," shouts a merry King Arthur, his outstretched arm spilling mead all over a large round table. "Sit at this here table of legend and tell me your tall tales of damsels in distress, witches and wizards, beasts and monsters, fire and ice, and courageous adventures from across my kingdom and beyond…"

With that, King Arthur jumps up and sits down in the middle of the table, a move that raises cheers from the assembled 25 knights of the realm. "And be quick, I am drunk!"

Sir Dagonet steps forward, a short and thin man with long hair and a fresh face.

"Ah, my jester knight!" laughs King Arthur. "And what tale do you have for my delight?"

"Well, sir, you know me," said Sir Dagonet. "I may not be as brave as Sir Lancelot… or as strong as Sir Galahad… or as cunning as Sir Percival… or as handsome as Sir Bedivere… or as charming as Sir Palamedes… or as tall as Sir Lamorak… or as quick as Sir Tristram… or as fat as Sir Leodegrance…"

The whole chorus of knights guffaws loudly and slams their tankards down on the table. Sir Leodegrance too, whose huge belly jiggles hypnotically.

"I may be none of these things, your Lord, but I am wise… perhaps the wisest in this council…"

"Well, steady on," interrupts Sir Ector, the wisest and oldest knight present.

Another round of laughter fills the massive room, the castle's finest, save for the throne.

"Sorry, Sir Ector, second wisest," Sir Dagonet continues. "I may have not been on any quests, or defeated any dragons, or rescued any princesses, or pulled swords from stones... but I do have a riddle for you all... an internal battle as complex as any quest. And whoever solves it can take my seat around the table... the closest to the king..."

At that, the half-sober knights all sit up.

To sit to the right of the king around this hallowed table is a privilege bestowed to the knight with the most recent, or most courageous, or most legendary, victory or kill in battle. Sir Dagonet always sits to the left of the king, a perk of being the jester.

Sir Dagonet sits down in his chair and leans forward, a motion replicated by the other knights around the table.

"There are three people sitting on the shore of a lake—Lucan, Mordred and Gareth," begins Sir Dagonet. "One of them is a brave knight, one is a knave, and one is a spy. The knight always tells the truth, of course. The knave always lies, naturally. And the spy, well, he can lie or tell the truth. Do you understand?"

All 50 ears are now listening intently to Sir Dagonet's every syllable, and all heads nod in unison. You can hear a pin drop.

"Lucan says, 'Gareth is a knave;' Mordred says, 'Lucan is a knight;' and Gareth says, 'I am the spy.' So, tell me, friends: Who is the knight, who is the knave, and who is the spy?"

"That's not a very funny joke," snorts King Arthur, who hasn't been paying attention.

"I know, sir... but it's a test..." Dagonet whispers to King Arthur, "to find out which of your brave knights is the smartest. Who will figure it out first, I wonder?"

Shields

*"The general who is skilled in defense hides
in the most secret recesses of the earth."*

"How many shields have you gone through this week, Nechtan?" asks the chieftain of the trusty Nechtan, who, as one of the senior warriors, is famed for his skills with sword and shield.

"Twenty-one, laird, 21 for sure," comes the reply from the grizzled veteran.

"And how many swords?" continues the laird.

"Six or more, laird."

"Good work," says the stocky fighter. "Keep it up."

"He must be one hell of a fighter," says Oisin to his partner, Niamh.

"Don't be silly, Nechtan hasn't fought for years now," comes the reply from the wise woman. "He's only got one arm, since he lost that one fighting the Robogdii last year."

How can this be so?

The Road to Rune

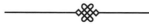

*"Let your plans be dark and impenetrable as night,
and when you move, fall like a thunderbolt."*

Thor, the god of warfare and thunder, kneeled as he held the near-lifeless body of his father, Odin, king of Asgard, in his arms. Around them swirled the chaos and noise of the great Ragnarök, a battle prophesied to be the beginning of the end for the Norse gods and their world as they knew it. Thor's brother, Loki, and his son, Fenrir, a giant wolf, had grown powerful. This was their war, and Fenrir had defeated and nearly devoured Odin in combat, much to Thor's growing grief and anger.

Before Odin slipped away into the celestial realm far from where Thor could gaze, Odin handed his mighty warrior son a handful of unsorted runes that made the Norse alphabet, Elder Futhark.

"Tell Asgard I am no longer king," Odin said. "Tell them this and believe it within."

Thor looked at the runes in his hands.

ᚦᚢᚱ ᛁᛉ ᚲᛁᛟ ᛁᛏᛉ ᚺᛡᛗᛗᛖᚱ ᛏᛁᛗᛗ

****

Days after Odin's passing, Thor placed the runes down on a table. It had been more than a millennium since Thor had read runes, the language of his elders. He would need a key.

He went to his father's chambers and collected a giant stone rune tablet. On it were the runes' symbols and translations. Thor got to work exercising his mind muscles for once.

ᚨ = A	ᛒ = B	ᛗ =D	ᛖ = E	ᚠ = F	ᚷ = G	ᚺ = H	ᛁ = I	ᛃ = J
ᚲ =K	ᛚ =L	ᛗ =M	ᚾ = N	◇ =Ng	ᛟ = O	ᛈ =P	ᚱ = R	ᛊ =S
		ᛏ =T	ᚦ = Th	ᚢ = U	ᛈ = W	ᛉ = Z		

Once translated, what did Odin's message say?

A Question of Order

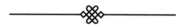

*"He who is skilled in attack flashes forth
from the topmost heights of heaven."*

Aengus, Balor, Cael, Diarmaid and Elouan ran into battle one after the other. Aengus charged in before Balor, but after Cael. Diarmaid rushed in screaming before Elouan but after Balor. What was the order of attack?

Odin's Whisper

"In order to defeat the enemy, our men must be roused to anger."

"Behold, I am your father!" shouted Odin to his army of legendary warriors, powerful and skilled fighters known for their extraordinary strength and uncontrollable rage in battle. "Everything you are… is because of me!"

Ragnar—Odin's number one Viking warrior, a man with unmatched ferocity, almost invincible on the battlefield in the Norse lands—threw up his arms and roared with anger. Such was Ragnar's power, it was believed that he was impervious to pain, even death, when roused to unthinkable anger. Every time a battle began, Ragnar was commanded—by a simple starting word—into a subconscious state so violent he struck fear into the hearts of Odin's opponents with unstoppable, relentless aggression.

Ragnar wasn't always angry, however. King Odin, father of Thor and the Norse worlds, was the only with the ability to trigger the beginning and end of the rage within Ragnar and his Viking brothers—and all it took was a single word. Enemies feared Ragnar so much that they wouldn't dare invade Odin's lands for fear of fierce retribution. Rarely did Odin use this fearsome word, of course, but all he had to do was whisper it into Gungnir, his powerful spear, and Ragnar and his fellow warriors would transform into incredible hulks until they heard the whispered word from Odin once more.

What was the word? You have been given all the clues in the words above.

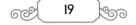

Plant Me a Kingdom

"The skillful leader overthrows the enemy's kingdom without lengthy operations in the field."

Old tales are told of the king who had no heir. The king, in his wisdom, decided to hand his kingdom and his power over to any honest, decent person who seemed worthy, and he devised a test to find such a person. To do this he came up with a plan: he offered a tiny seed to everyone in the kingdom, declaring that the throne would be handed to the one who grew the finest tree after five years. Five years later, the castle was filled with trees of all shapes and sizes, some enormous, some wispy and some even bearing fruit. How would the king decide? Strangely, one girl was there with a simple pot filled with earth and nothing else. The king awarded the kingdom to her there and then. Why?

The Wicked Woods

*"Movement amongst the trees of a forest
shows that the enemy is advancing."*

Merlin, the great wizard of legend, and a teenage Arthur, future king of England, are walking together one beautiful summer's day. Ahead lies a forest. Arthur stops in his tracks. He is scared. He has heard whispers of the evil that haunts these woods, a place where ancient wars are still waged between demons and devils and all who dare enter.

"I'm not going in there," says Arthur, shaking and pointing. "It's the Wicked Woods."

Merlin looks at his young companion and walks on towards the treeline.

"Fear not going *into* the forest, Arthur. It is easily defeated," the wizard says, encouraging the boy who would be king to walk forward.

"How so?" asks Arthur, standing still like a sword in a stone.

"Think about it," says the wise one as he vanishes between the trees.

Why should Arthur not be scared?

Half a Sheep

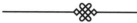

*"To see victory only when it is within the ken
of the common herd is not the acme of excellence."*

A shepherd had 16 sheep and would keep them near his hut in groups of four so he could see them out of each window.

One night, the naughty soldiers from the local garrison thought they'd prepare for a feast, so during the night they stole away with half the herd. However, to avoid trouble from the shepherd, they ensured that he would still be able to see four sheep from each window of his hut. How could this be?

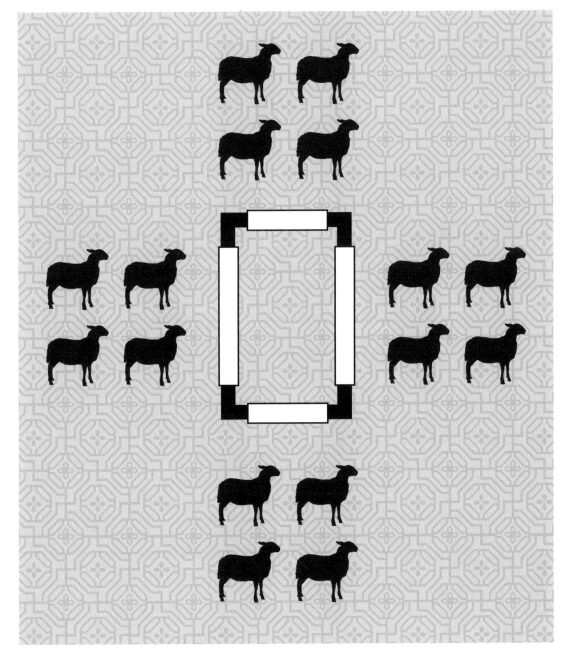

Negotiations

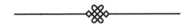

"The skillful strategist defeats the enemy without doing battle."

Preparing for a "peaceful negotiation" with an aggressive territory in the west, the Emperor ordered his Grand Commandant to increase the army's military capacity to 100 *shuangshou* per month and for an accompanying expansion in training and recruitment of volunteers to wield this deadly, two-handed, double-edged sword. The following month, at the next military court conference, the Emperor asked the Grand Commandant (incidentally, it was a position held until death, and the current incumbent was hoping that would be a few years more), "Has the manufacturing capacity increased to 100 swords?" The surprisingly loud, proud reply boomed out across the court: "No, your excellency." The other bystanders looked down, and they could have heard a jade hairpin drop and shatter.

But instead of hurrying the appointment of a new Grand Commandant, thus spelling the demise of the current holder of that position, the Emperor saw fit to reward him with an increased salary-rank to 700-*dan*. Why?

Orders!

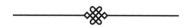

*"Maneuvering with an army is advantageous;
with an undisciplined multitude, most dangerous."*

While orders were being distributed by the centurion to his men, two Roman legionnaires stood at the back, not paying much attention. Their *decanus* had been taken ill that morning, so discipline at the rear was slack, almost playful. As the troops broke to return to their tents, Flavius turned to Parthius and said, "Answer me this if you can: What am I talking about? I can hear it, it controls me and I will do as it says and so will you. But nobody can see it, nobody has ever seen it, and nobody will ever see it."

Parthius paused and thought for a moment before he continued on his way. "I have no idea," he said. "That doesn't sound like anything I've encountered." But he had, and when Flavius told him the answer, he laughed. What was it?

Hats Off to You

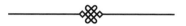

*"Method & Discipline:
one of the five constant factors."*

Captured by the Sumerians, four prisoners of war are buried in sand and left to the ants in the burning sun. However, feeling generous, their captor, Ugula Hazi, decides that if one of the prisoners displays good sense, and employs the right method, he will release them all and allow them to join *his* army. The prisoners are in a line—Adamen, Biluda, Dagrim and Enkara—all facing the same way (Adamen can see Biluda and Dagrim; Biluda can only see Dagrim). There is a large block of stone between Dagrim and Enkara, so Enkara cannot see any of the others, nor be seen by them. Ugula Hazi takes four hats from a sack at random—two black (on Biluda and Enkara) and two white (on Adamen and Dagrim). He places them on the heads of the prisoners and says, "If anyone can tell me the hue of their hat within a count of 10, I will release you all." After just a few moments, which prisoner is able to figure out the hue of their hat?

Warrior Count

*"What the ancients called a clever fighter
is one who not only wins, but excels
in winning with ease."*

Unga the chieftain looks around at his brave warriors after years of conflict and battle. He counts the warriors and notices that all except two have lost fingers, all except two use spears, and all except two have lost an eye. How many warriors does he have?

Choices

"The Commander stands for the virtue of wisdom."

"The slaves are revolting!" Beneath the circus maximus there's a minor uprising under way. Doomed to failure from the start, that doesn't stop Cato, who has simply had enough of this life... there must be more. As part of his escape, Cato rounds a corner and almost falls over his old friend Trophimus, who is lying on the floor, fatally wounded by a soldier's spear. "Keep going... to freedom," Trophimus says to Cato, pointing to three identical doors. "The first one leads to the guardroom... I don't know if anyone is still in there or not." He gasps for breath. "The second leads to the sewers—crocodiles in there..." he continues, "and behind the third door is the Emperor's lion, who has not eaten for a month... Choose wisely, my friend... goodbye."

Which door should Cato choose to go through?

Diadema

"The best thing of all is to take the enemy's country whole and intact; to shatter and destroy it is not so good."

In 53 BC, the Battle of Carrhae rages between the Roman Republic and the Parthian Empire. The Roman army is led by the immensely wealthy and powerful Marcus Licinius Crassus. The Parthian forces are led by General Surena. When Crassus's Roman forces are outsmarted and suffer a decisive defeat, the whole army is taken hostage, and Crassus is captured by the Parthians. At night, Crassus and Surena meet to negotiate the terms of his release…

"I will let you and your army go, Crassus, if you pay my exorbitant ransom and return the captured Roman territories—and solemnly swear to never attack or interfere with Parthia again," says Surena. "Furthermore, you must wear this Parthian Crown with a diadem at all times, for total public humiliation."

"Never!" shouts the chained Crassus, spitting at his rival.

"Fine," replies Surena. "Then you will die as you have lived. I'll put your money where your mouth is!"

Surena then speaks one terrifying word: "Aurum."

Crassus gulps.

What does Surena mean? And how does Crassus die?

Transformation

"Earth: one of the five constant factors."

On a hard march south from the port of Ptolemais Theron, the legion was hot, quiet and subdued. Nobody knew what to expect from this barren landscape, so different from the olive groves of home. But this was the legion and every man knew his place and purpose. Titus was renowned as a bit of an entertainer when the time was right, but knew the moments he could get away with speaking—and those he couldn't. Sometimes he would set a riddle that would rumble through the entire cohort. Usually it was in the evening as the soldiers ate around a fire before turning in for the night. This time, he offered his question to his marching companions:

"Pulled from deep, when heated I weep,
Burned and beaten, I kill for a living.
What am I?"

Riddle Me This

"If you know yourself but not the enemy,
for every victory gained you will also suffer a defeat."

After a long day's march, Maximus and Marius find themselves sheltering from the rain on a windy moor in the north of Britannia. The cohort is forced to stay where they are because of the inclement weather. The two soldiers are not worried about this; much greater problems await them at the border with Hibernia. To pass the time, Marius comes up with the following riddle:

"I am foremost in victory, I have never tasted defeat.
I am found in the midst of gravity, but absent from Earth or the Moon.
You can find me in the middle of any river, and I'm always in love.
I was sent to the grave and ended up in heaven… What am I?"

Can you figure out what he is talking about?

BRITANNIA
et
HIBERNIA.

BRITANNIA PTOLEMAEI.

BRITANNIA STRABONIS.

HADRIANI MVRVS.

Cassiterides, Silurum,
Sylinae Iae.

Cleopatra's Dilemma

"Do not swallow bait offered by the enemy."

Cleopatra, the last ruler of Egypt's Ptolemaic kingdom, found herself facing a conundrum. She was in love with two men: Marcus Antonius and Julius Caesar, the great Roman generals and statesmen. It was a complicated, and powerful, love triangle. Cleopatra loved them both equally, but knew she must decide between the two or fear losing them both, as well as her queendom.

Alone in her goat's-milk bath one evening, the queen pondered the pros and cons of both her lovers. They were both gifted with great intellect and oratory powers. So Cleopatra devised an ingenious word square for them both to solve. Cleopatra had heard that word squares were all the rage after a man named Sator carved one into stone in Pompeii. His read *Sator Arepo tenet opera rotas,* but Cleopatra was sure she could come up with a better one.

"The first to solve my love square," Cleopatra said aloud to her goat companion, "would gain my heart—and end the love triangle!"

To help the two generals in their efforts, Cleopatra also sent a few clues.

1. Not a triangle or square, love is an endless…
2. Lands of Spain and Portugal together.
3. Make new coins from old.
4. Back away in fear.
5. Stay longer in my presence.
6. Consumers of food.

X	X	X	X	X	X
X	X	X	X	X	X
X	X	X	X	X	X
X	X	X	X	X	X
X	X	X	X	X	X
X	X	X	X	X	X

Making More...

"It is only one who is thoroughly acquainted with the evils of war that can thoroughly understand the profitable way of carrying it on."

Leonardo sells weapons to the state during peacetime as the country gears up for war. During actual wartime the demand for his wares goes up; he sells more and makes more profit. It's hard to keep track, though, so he decides to employ a new way of setting and keeping track of his prices. He writes down the following:

1, 1, 2, 3, 5, 8, 13

What comes next in his sequence, and what is the logic behind it?

Triangulation

"The onset of troops is like the rush of a torrent which will even roll stones along in its course."

Looking at his plans, the Emperor realizes he must turn his army around to face the other direction. If the soldiers simply turn around, they will lose their formation and be more open to attack. His aide-de-camp places six coins on the table as shown, and between them they figure out the minimum number of coins to move in order to change direction completely. How many, and which, coins must be moved?

Cost of Living

*"High prices cause the people's
substance to be drained away."*

Many members of the population of Rome have noticed that prices have been steadily rising during wartime. The cost of tomatoes has gone up, olive oil is costlier, and herbs and salt are commanding higher prices than ever before. Cassius has been keeping track, as he is worried about civil insurrection that could destabilize the army. Looking at the grid he has noted, can you figure out the missing price at the end, and what the logic behind the sequence is?

3	12	33
4	10	36
6	7	36
5	9	??

Wishes

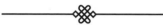

*"The clever combatant imposes his will on the enemy,
but does not allow the enemy's will to be imposed on him."*

The ancient warrior Akinnad had endured much conflict in his time. He had seen victory, tasted defeat, and witnessed magic and mystery besides. But this time he feared his story was at an end. Surrounded by 100 foes, he and two men were all that was left of the defending force.

To the surprise and delight of the grizzled warmaker, a local djinn appeared and granted Akinnad one wish, but it came with a condition. Whatever he wished for would be granted double to the advancing enemy.

What did Akinnad wish for?

There Will Be Blood

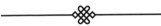

"The general who wins a battle makes many calculations in his temple ere the battle is fought."

Julian the Apostate served as a Roman Emperor from 361 AD to 363 AD. He was the only Roman general to have died after being wounded by an arrow. This arrow did not fly through the air, however. It was plunged into his chest at close range by one of his five closest advisors, each of whom was desperate to take over from their leader. They were:

1. Cornelia Marcellus
2. Decimus Pompeius
3. Fabiana Tiberia
4. Quintus Valerii
5. Lucius Antonius

After yanking the arrow out of his own chest cavity, Julian fell down to the hard stone of the temple. With his last few breaths, as the blood drained from his brain to his bloodied nib, Julian, a great mathematician, etched a clue to the identity of the murderer guilty of stabbing him into the stone:

$$X V I I$$
$$X X I I$$

Julian's assassin was eventually caught and executed. Who was it?

Time to Think

"The Commander stands for the virtue of strictness."

Amir Al-Farid Al-Mansur, a brutal commander in the Umayyad Caliphate, under the ruler of Muawiyah I in 8th-century Arabia, was a precise and disciplined man, infamous for never wasting time. Not a second.

On the day before his army's invasion of Constantinople in 717, Al-Mansur spoke to his gathered generals and told them he wanted to besiege the city at exactly 3 o'clock in the morning. Not a second earlier or later.

Al-Mansur decreed that he wanted "a surprise attack."

There was just one problem. It would be too dark to tell the time. And sundials could not tell the time in the dark, or even in moonlight.

One of Al-Mansur's most trusted generals, Famir, told his commander not to worry. He had been gifted a new invention by an acquaintance: an hourglass. Two, to be precise.

"It tells the time using sand," Famir said.

These new devices greatly excited the precise and disciplined general. "These are perfect," he said, gasping at their accuracy.

"The only problem," said Famir, "is that one measures time in seven-minute portions… and one measures time in 11-minute segments."

Al-Mansur stroked his long beard and pondered. "How to do this?" he puzzled. "Aha! I know!"

At 15 minutes before sundown that day, Al-Mansur told the time from his trusted sundial for the final time at precisely 6.45pm. He then instructed two soldiers to measure out 15 minutes between the two hourglasses precisely until 3 o'clock the next morning. Then, and only then, would the invasion begin.

What did Al-Mansur instruct the soldiers to do?

Centurions

*"When the soldiers stand leaning on their spears,
they are faint from want of food."*

Five centurions stood guard at the bottom of Golgotha 2,000 years ago. They were awaiting a chorus of crucifixions to gather at their spot, no doubt sun-scorched and exhausted. The centurions' job was simply to point the poor people with crosses up the hill. It had been ages, though, and no one had come through.

"This is dull," said Cassius, the lead soldier of this little legion. "It's too hot for crucifixion today."

Aelius and Belenus, leaning on their spears, nodded their heads in agreement, trying desperately not to fall asleep.

Just then, two other centurions, Decimus and Egnatius, ran up to their colleagues.

"Look, I found some apples," said Decimus. "I was starving."

Decimus handed each of the other four hungry men an apple.

"Let's have a race," said Cassius, excited. "The first one to finish gets to rest their legs until the first victim arrives."

With that, all five centurions bit into their apples eagerly.

Aelius finished before Cassius, but behind Decimus.

Decimus finished before Aelius, but after Belenus.

Cassisus did not come last.

"So, who won?" asked Egnatius, picking apple from his teeth.

Brothers in Arms

"An army without its baggage-train is lost."

In 737, an Abbasid civil war broke out between two brothers, Caliph Harun, al-Rashid, and his younger brother, al-Hadi. They were fighting over land, as brothers tend to do.

The battle took place in Raqqa (modern-day Syria). At the end of the two-month siege, al-Hadi's forces were defeated. The moment of victory came when al-Rashid sent fighters to expose and attack al-Hadi's baggage trains, wagons containing supplies, munitions and explosives. Without them, al-Hadi had nothing.

The following day, after the battle's end, al-Rashid sent a messenger with a bag to meet his brother. Inside the bag was a note. It was a list:

Kafroun
Edlib
Ebla
Palmyra
Tartus
Homs
Ez-Zabadani
Baniyas
Aleppo
Ghouta

Al-Hadi looked at the note and told his servant to pack his bags. He was going on a long trip. Or was he?

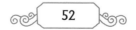

Kafroun
Edlib
Ebla
Palmyra
Tartus
Homs
Ez-Zabadani
Baniyas
Aleppo
Ghouta

Leofric and Godiva

"The worst policy of all is to besiege walled cities."

Lord Leofric, the Earl of Mercia and Lord of Bristol, and his wife, Godiva, stood tall in a turret atop a large brick-wall gate, the highest viewpoint in Bristol's famously walled city. On this particular clear and dry night, the couple were bored and looking to spend some quality time together, so they gave the two guards on duty the night off. They hoped to spend the evening looking out across their land and the people they ruled, gazing into each other's eyes under a blanket of stars, and drinking merrily from a flagon of mead.

Romance was soon thwarted, however, when a scruffy young intruder turned up at the gate, demanding to be let into the city.

"Let me in!" he shouted up to Leofric and Godiva, unaware of their true identities. "I must enter immediately!"

Godiva shouted down, "Where are you from, boy?"

"Coventry," he replied. "But the taxes are too high! I can no longer live there… and my debtors are in pursuit."

Godiva and Leofric looked at each other and took pity on the young man.

"Do you have any gold?" Leofric shouted down.

"No, sir, I have none!"

Leofric and Godiva were not of a mind to let any uneducated and uncouth ruffians and scoundrels into their city—Bristol had too many already.

"I've got an idea," said Lady Godiva to her husband. "Bear with me," she told him with a wink.

"To enter the walled city, you must know the law!" Godiva shouted down.

"A law?" shouted up the young man.

"There is only one law," Godiva replied. "To accept it is to gain access."

"What is it?" the boy yelled, growing impatient.

Godiva laughed, and shouted down:

"There is a toll, but no charge.
There is a door, but no entrance.
There is a hurry, but no time.
There is a battle, but no war.
There is only one law."

"What is the law?" Lady Godiva asked. "Say it... and you can enter!"

A Caged Lion

"Captured soldiers should be kindly treated and kept."

At the end of the Crusades, King Richard of England, beloved by his subjects as Richard the Lionheart, was captured by Leopold V, Duke of Austria, near Vienna. He was subsequently handed over to the Holy Roman Emperor, Henry VI. Richard was imprisoned in the castle of Dürnstein, situated on the Danube River in modern-day Austria. He was held captive there for more than a year.

Blondel de Nesle, a troubadour and minstrel who was known to be a close friend of Richard, reportedly set out from France to find the imprisoned king. He went from castle to castle, singing a specific song that only Richard and Blondel knew. The song had a distinctive tune, and lyrics that had personal significance to the two of them.

According to legend, while singing the song outside the walls of Dürnstein Castle, Blondel heard Richard singing along from within the castle walls. Recognizing the tune and the response, Blondel was able to confirm that Richard was indeed held captive there.

Blondel then devised a cunning plan. He bribed one of the Austrian prison guards by telling him that one of his prisoners was the King of England—richer than even Henry VI. Blondel then told the guard his plan.

"Lion," the guard told Richard, placing down a cup of water on the stone floor. "On the fourteenth night, be ready to pounce."

Richard, hungry and malnourished, had no idea what the guard meant, but knew that if Blondel was close, so too was his freedom.

That first night, the guard brought Richard a *karrote* to eat. The next he took Richard some *erbse*; the next he brought Richard some *ysop*, all of which he pronounced in his thick Austrian accent as he handed the food to his prisoner, words Richard could barely understand. The guard continued to bring Richard local fruits, vegetables, herbs and spices—*urdbohne, nuss, dill, endivie, radieschen, salbei, thymian, olive, nelke* and *eiche*—giving Richard all the nutrients, energy—and information—he needed to escape. How?

Golden Ratio

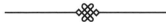

*"Do not interfere with an army
that is returning home after a loss."*

Leonardo of Pisa—or Fibonacci, as he was known to his best friends—was staring out his bedroom window. Through this frame of reference, he could see all of life, and all its beauty, as a chronological kaleidoscope, a sequence of subsequent numbers the sum of the two preceding ones. Everywhere he went, everywhere he looked, everything he touched, these same numbers appeared in his mind's eye: 0, 1, 1, 2, 3, 5, 8, 13, 21, and on and on it went.

"I am bored of this sequence of numbers!" Fibonacci shouted out his window to anyone who would listen. "I'd give anything for a numerological intervention to distract my mind!"

As these words floated out the window, down below a soldier, battered and bruised from battle, looked up.

"I know one," he said.

"Come up and share, good fellow!" replied Fibonacci.

Upstairs, the tired and beleaguered soldier sat down.

"Tell me," began Fibonacci. "Are you a Guelph or a Ghibelline?"

"A Guelph," the soldier answered. "But I return home now."

Fibonacci nodded his head. "I am sorry for your loss."

"Tell me your numbers, soldier," said Fibonacci. "I dream to hear them."

"I will," said the soldier, thumbing through pages of notes titled *Liber Abaci.* "In return for a bed, a bath and a meal."

"Indeed, you shall feast, be clean and rest well!" said Fibonacci, springing to his feet. The soldier grabbed a quill and ink and began to scribble.

Employ 8 exactly 8 times to equal 1,000.

"That's it?" Fibonacci asked, grabbing the parchment.

"Yes," said the soldier. "You may use only addition, subtraction, multiplication and division."

With that, the soldier promptly fell asleep.

What is the solution?

Jest a Minute

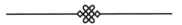

"Five Dangerous Faults:
Recklessness, which leads to destruction."

"We must attack now! The enemy is weak and retreating!" Frank Van Hallen, one of the king's most trusted servants, was thirsting for blood. The French had been convincingly defeated after their siege of Auberoche Castle had been broken by the king's ally, Sir John of Hawkwood, who had trekked his forces up from Italy. "Patience, my good knight... we will wait to see where the enemy gathers and attack them with force once and for all. We'll not chase them through the forest like dogs on a truffle hunt." The king spoke, and the knights listened. "Jester, a pass-time!" He gestured toward his No. 1 jester, Orlando le Pettus, who had been chewing on a roasted leg of swan in the hope that he would not be called upon.

"Yes, my liege," came the reply after a hearty belch, and the jester approached the group. Facing up to Van Hallen, he spoke loud and clear:

"Answer me this, brave knight: What is it that comes only once per year—but once in every year for sure—once per season, but you will never see it in a month, and there are none in the past!"

Van Hallen was stumped, and annoyed.

What is the answer?

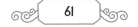

Deduction

"Knowledge of the enemy's dispositions can only be obtained from other men."

In the Forest of Sherwood roam two types of men: noble knights, who always tell the truth; and Merry Men, who always lie. The Sheriff of Nottingham has rounded up two men and cannot tell what they are. One of them says, "We are both Merry Men!" Is this true?

valiente

tlaocçtlacatl

What Do You See?

"To see the sun and moon is no sign of sharp sight."

Moving by night to avoid the Spanish invaders who have poured onto the shores for many moons now, the warrior Guatemoc and his brother are making their way through the jungle to warn chief Tlacaelel of the impending invasion. The two have witnessed firsthand the damage that foreigners can bring through disease, greed and numerical and technological superiority. "But we have our ways," says Guatemoc. The brothers have to keep their wits about them, and as they wait for night to fall, Guatemoc says to his brother, "I bet the Spanish would never be able to answer me by telling me what this could be... can you?" And he continues: "You can see him under the sun. He is there under the moon. He follows you wherever you go, but may disappear in an instant. He can dance, jump and run but never speaks. Who is he?"

Tlacaelel is stumped but doesn't want to admit it, and the two walk in silence for some way. Suddenly, his face lights up, and he tells Guatemoc the correct answer. What is it?

Logistics

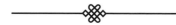

"Use not your troops unless there is something to be gained."

Following the mayhem of battle at Agincourt, Thomas de Malo was returning home. He was one of the lucky ones not killed or taken prisoner by the accursed English, led by that dreadful King Henry, who was taking his claim to the French throne seriously. Thomas had had enough; he had his faithful attack dog Jérôme with him, which was probably the only reason he was alive. The battle was humiliating and the aftermath a bloodbath as those English savages executed the prisoners. Whatever happened to the tradition of demanding a ransom? Thomas's journey back to his safe haven of Rennes was long and perilous; anyone could be an enemy, with political division carving up the country in the wake of that battle.

Thomas had been hiding beside a riverbank for the whole day. It was the last river he needed to cross, and he was already looking forward to eating eggs from the chicken he'd found along the route and the cheese he'd bought that morning with his last *deniers*. But his path across the river Vilaine was blocked. It was late, and the boatman had long since departed, leaving his ferry chained to the jetty. Thomas would have to make his way across in the only craft he could find: a rickety, leaky, one-man rowboat. He could only carry himself and one other creature at a time, and he couldn't leave the dog with the chicken, or the chicken with the cheese, because hunger would get the best of either of them. How did he get all across to the other side without incident?

The Cellar Door

*"One cartload of the enemy's provisions
is equivalent to twenty of one's own."*

"Fawkes, are you listening?" Robert asked the man, who appeared not to be listening at all but instead admiring the barrels of gunpowder at his feet. "Hello, Guido?"

Guido—or Guy, as he was also known to his gang of rebels—came back into the room and refocused his attention.

"Guy, it's important to me that I know that this gunpowder remains in this room *at all times*, do you understand?" Robert continued. "It's of extreme value. The very future of England depends on you guarding this gunpowder in this cellar—you understand that, yes?"

"I do, Catesby," said Guy. "But if you could tell me again, I'd be much obliged, sir."

Robert Catesby rolled his eyes. He didn't have time to explain his master plan *again*. It was a complicated plot. Guy was a clever man, but no match for Robert. And besides, Robert needed to be elsewhere. Somewhere less... explosive... than below the House of Lords.

"Guy," said Robert, frustrated, "I've masterminded—you know what, I'm just going to lock you in... so you can't go anywhere and ruin my plan."

With that, Robert attached a nine-digit lock to the door of the cellar. Then, with a quill, he scribbled on a piece of paper the numbers 1 6 4 9 7 _ _ _ _.

"This is called a lock, Guy. It's a brand-new invention, a popular new way of retaining objects. By the time you figure out the next four numbers in the sequence, you'll have just enough time to light the fuses, come upstairs and, well, watch the fireworks. OK?"

Guy nodded. Robert handed Guy the piece of paper and started to walk upstairs.

"Oh, and one more thing, Guy," Robert said, turning around. "It's probably best if you don't smoke tobacco around the gunpowder. Don't want you to go up in flames like some bonfire, do we now?"

And with that Robert Catesby ran up a stone staircase.

Guy looked down at the piece of paper and pondered.

What were the four final numbers in the sequence?

Cheers!

*"He will win whose army is animated by
the same spirit throughout all its ranks."*

Minutes before the battle, the commander gives a speech to rouse his troops, who are about to charge in. Two brave warriors stand at the back, listening intently. At the end the commander says, "Now, time for our special cheer," and continues, "Let's raise a shout or three to the gods, in our unique way." He then shouts "ONE!" and the fighters cheer three times. He shouts "TWO!" and the troops cheer three times. He shouts "THREE!" and is greeted by five cheers. How many cheers are there when he shouts "FOUR!"?

Hunting Time

*"Bring war material with you from home,
but forage from the enemy."*

Camping out, waiting for what would become known as the Battle of Shiloh to start, the men are getting restless. They could be waiting for weeks for the action to get going. Sergeant Flores gives permission for some of the soldiers to go hunting. But there is a condition: there is a legend that tells of the best time to hunt. It is a time hidden in a word that reads the same forwards, backwards, up and down. If the men can figure out the word, they can go hunting. What is the word?

Rearranging the Lines

"Do not attack soldiers whose temper is keen."

Minutes before the attack is due, the general looks at his front line of troops. He sees them arranged alternately, as in the image opposite. This will never do—those two types of fighter do not mix well, so must be separated in order to cause greater fear and damage to the enemy. But each type does not like to be left alone, so two adjacent soldiers must be moved at a time. Can you figure out how the general separates the ranks in only three moves?

Final Words

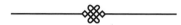

"The Commander stands for the virtue
of sincerity."

"I've been shot," whispers Lord Horatio Nelson, raising his right hand to his still-smoking left shoulder. He collapses hard and fast onto the quarterdeck of his ship, the *HMS Victory.* "Damned… French… musket…"

Colonel Edward Berry runs over to his beloved commander. "No!" he screams. Berry picks him up and drags him below deck to see the ship's medic, William Beatty. All Beatty can do is shake his head.

"It's OK, my friends," whispers Nelson to Beatty and Berry. "England is saved."

Nelson takes Berry's forearm tight, and with conviction, squeezes it. "Quick, too map, hand that me," he speaks, out of order. "Scrambles my mind my fate before."

Berry pulls a chart of the known world from the table within reach and hands it to Nelson, ripping off a small piece as he does. Nelson then grabs a quill from the table, dips it into his bleeding shoulder, and writes on the torn map. He then hands it to his loyal second-in-command. "Emma this hand to note—promise me, Berry. Needs it Horatia."

Nelson then thrusts the blood-soaked map into the palm of Berry's hand.

"What is it?" whispers Berry into Nelson's ear.

"Home," croaks Nelson, coughing blood up and out from his lungs. "Thank God… I have… done my… duty."

With that, Nelson slips into unconsciousness. Berry places the note inside his jacket pocket, and hangs his head low.

****

Hours later, as the bittersweet news spreads of Nelson's victory at the Battle of Trafalgar, and the nation mourns the loss of its greatest naval commander, Berry, alone aboard the *HMS Victory*, standing over Nelson's Spanish charts and maps, takes the blood-stained note from his jacket and unfolds it. It reads:

N.P. LATECOMER

"What on earth could this mean?" says Berry, scratching his chin.

Can you figure it out?

A Glass Half Full

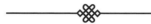

"The skillful leader subdues the enemy's troops without any fighting."

April 18, 1775

"Where are the enemy?" yells General Alexander to one of his loyal riflemen, a man named Jones.

"They are advancing, General. They will be with us by morning, weather permitting," replies Jones, trying his best to stop his nervous stutter from making an appearance. "T-T-They've crossed the border and are firmly on their way. Small teams of snipers have been unable to keep them at bay. Our eagles are watching in the field… but they're quick as dogs. Too quick."

"Dammit!" yells Alexander, slamming his fist down on his chart table inside his makeshift command tent. He takes a glug of brown water from a battle-scarred glass and then spits it out. Alexander brings the glass up to his face.

"This isn't rum—what is it?"

"It's w-w-w-water, sir, from Kentucky," replies Alexander's second-in-command, a colonel by the name of Kirkpatrick.

"It's disgusting—bring me rum and only rum."

"Yes, sir, at once," Kirkpatrick storms out the tent.

Outside the tent, the general's exhausted and ill men, approximately 100 reserves, pause for sustenance after a long trek across the wilderness of lands soon to be called free.

"How are the men, Jones? Be direct with me…"

"Many are unwell—50 or more, sir, overwhelming exhaustion. It's slowing them down. No clean water and running low on provisions."

At that moment, Kirkpatrick storms into the tent holding a large flagon of rum.

"Here you go, sir, rum fresh from the barrel. I'm afraid it's the last, sir."

"Dammit!" Alexander yells, slamming his fist down on the table again. "How can I lead my men to victory if I have no rum? Is there no good news, Jones?"

"Well, sir, there is some. The enemy—more than 500 men—have stopped downstream of us on the east bank, for now, s-s-sir," stutters Jones, trying to perk his commander up. "For nightfall, presumably by the stream that runs parallel to the river. They are covered by canopy—our eagles on the bank cannot tell us any more."

Alexander mops his brow with a sweat-soaked cloth. "We must slow them down," the general says into his collar. "Otherwise…"

Suddenly, an explosion goes off outside Alexander's tent. Small enough to not raise concern, but loud enough for—

"What on earth was that?" Alexander yells.

"It's the riflemen, sir. They're testing out the new powder that's just arrived by wagon. It's deadly stuff! They have sent too much—we'll have to bury what we can't carry."

"What a waste of good gunpowder," scowls Kirkpatrick as he pours his general a shot of rum.

Alexander picks up the glass and goes to drink it, but instead looks at it with more curiosity than a cat. He puts the glass down.

"Wait, Jones… I have an idea. Tell me… the wind… how does it blow?"

What does he have in mind?

Letters from Abroad

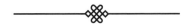

"There is no instance of a country having benefited from prolonged warfare."

My dearest Emily,

I have gone crazy without your love. It kept me sane from the start of this infernal war—but will it end? Do you still love me? You must! Otherwise, I am already dead. My heart is divided by these words, of course. How many months it has been since you kissed me last. I can no longer count the days. If only this war was as short as this letter, I would be home tomorrow, but the Empire needs me until the end.

Your husband, John

How long, in years, has John's war endured? And which war is it?

Finders Keepers

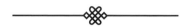

*"When you plunder a countryside,
let the spoil be divided amongst your men."*

In a faraway field, amidst the gunshot echoes of the Battle of Yorktown still raging in the background, two weary soldiers, Swigert and Cable, trudged along, their uniforms bloodied and their faces scorched with extreme fatigue. Their rifles had long since been thrown to the ground. The hot Virginia sun cast long shadows across the prairie, a reminder of the dark reality these pacifists faced. Heroes to some. Deserters to most. As they plodded along a dusty path toward uncertainty, Cable's eyes caught a glint of something metallic up ahead.

"What's that?" he exclaimed, bending down to look closer. He brushed away the dirt to reveal two weathered English coins, the image of a monarch's profile almost worn away on both.

Swigert's eyes widened with the realization of a treasure found. "English coins? Must've been dropped by one of the other side," he puzzled.

Cable nodded, turning the coin over in his hand. "Aye, but what's it doing all the way out here in the field? The battle is a long way distant."

As the two soldiers gazed at the coins, an idea formed collectively in their minds.

"You know," Cable began, "how about a little wager?"

"A wager?" Swigert said with a raised eyebrow.

"Indeed," Cable grinned. "A simple coin toss to decide who gets to keep the coins. A bit of much-needed relief from the battling, wouldn't you say?"

Swigert agreed. His friend had first found the coins and assumed they were his to keep, but here in these lands those coins had little value.

"A coin toss it is, then," Swigert said, excited. "But let's make it interesting. I've got an idea…"

Swigert took both coins in his hand. "I'll flip both the coins at the same time. You call heads or tails. If both coins show the same side—either both heads or both tails—I win. If the coins show different sides (one head and one tail), you win. First to five keeps the coins."

Cable nodded and watched his friend flip.

What should Cable's strategy for winning be?

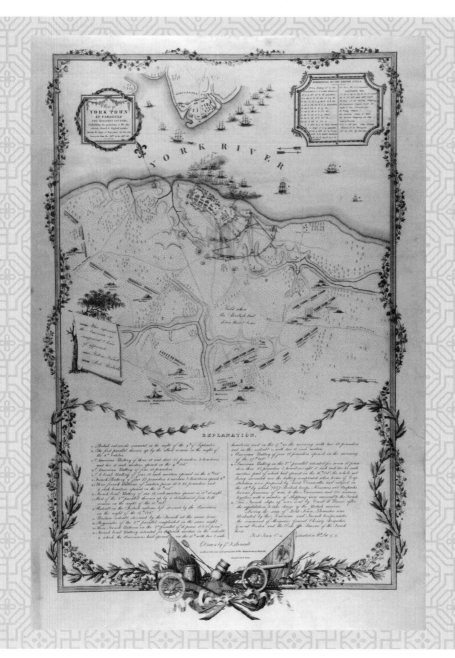

Light in the Night

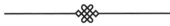

*"The skillful leader captures the enemy's cities
without laying siege to them."*

Creeping through Yorktown, sergeant J. Nick Johnston paused for breath. His mission seemed difficult to start with, but since the rest of his comrades were shot or captured, it had turned into a simple quest for survival. He was shivering from the freezing rain and, after crawling through a muddy field and two hedges, he was tired, hungry and filthy. He had tried all the doors in the narrow street; finally one opened, and in he stumbled. He found himself in a dark room, but could just make out a table. On it was a box of matches, a paraffin lamp and a candle. Close by was a wood stove with what looked like paper and kindling in it. There was only one match in the box, so what did the shivering soldier light first to ensure his survival?

Wasting Time

*"When the army is restless and distrustful,
trouble is sure to come from the other feudal princes."*

The generals sat in the tent and waited. It was a hot day; the sun beat down relentlessly. The men were restless, the generals even more so. They wanted the men to ride into battle, to face their foes and—ideally—to win. But they had to wait, for the orders to attack were still not through. As they goaded each other and studied the map once more, General Swanson set this puzzle for General Dwyer:

"Four eyes have I but cannot see; can you guess what I might be?"

None of the others could figure out what he was going on about, and by the time they did, the orders were in to take their minds off it: Charge! Can you solve the riddle?

Frenemies

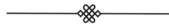

"One may know how to conquer without being able to do it."

The Duke of Wellington looked out at the sea of people, their faces full of admiration. "We were of course born in the same year, he and I, 1769," Wellington said of his great foe, Napoleon Bonaparte. "Napoleon a child of the Revolution, carried away by it and its success; I believe his object was the glory of France, and the consolidation of his own power," he continued. "And while, of course, we despised each other on the oceans and battlefields, we admired each other's skills. I certainly did his, and I used what I knew of his skills to defeat him at Waterloo."

A thunderous roar of applause echoed around the large banquet hall, a stateroom filled with dignitaries, royalty and admiralty from several nations friendly to the British flag.

"I used to say of him that his presence on the field made the difference of 40,000 men," Wellington continued, "and if I had taken 40,000 men to the field, I never would have been beaten."

Wellington stopped speaking for a second to lap up another loud crowd of cheers.

"Forty!" he called out. "Forty! Such was Napoleon's all-conquering might. But I beat that devil at his own game."

Wellington then paused for thought. Forty—forty—he thought to himself.

Wellington had said the word so many times in his head now he had semantic satiation—the word sounded strange and unfamiliar in his head, almost as if it had become disconnected from its meaning.

"Forty," Wellington said again out loud without realizing. "Of course, the reason I said '40,000 men' just then was deliberate. There is something special about the number 40 that I happen to love. It is unique in one way."

Silence filled the room. Wellington could have heard a pin drop.

"Can anyone guess what it is?"

Can you?

A Burning Question

"You may advance and be absolutely irresistible,
if you make for the enemy's weak points."

On the battlefield not far outside Maratha, Grenadier Callis was given his orders. "Wait 45 minutes until 12 o'clock, and then open fire. The advance troops will be in position by then, giving us an element of surprise and the chance of a swift victory. If you are early, you will give the game away. If you are late, the risk of failure of the attack is greatly increased. So, 45 minutes, no less, no more. Do you have a watch, Grenadier?"

"Yes sir, but—"

"Then use it!" The general cut him off, pulled on the reins of his horse and thundered off down the rough mountain path.

When the general departed, Callis took the pocket watch he had found two weeks previously on a corpse. Peeking through the cracked glass he could see that the rusty hands showed two minutes to midday (or midnight); it hadn't moved a tick in four days.

"We are done for, lads," sighed Callis. "Not to mention the others."

"Don't worry, sir," piped up the young Private Smee. "We've got two long fuses that burn for an hour each. Granted, they don't burn evenly, but they do burn for the hour. It's all we need."

"But how are we to know they are three-quarters done if the burn isn't even?" asked Callis, not unreasonably.

"Don't worry, sir, pass me the match," said Smee.

How do Grenadier Callis and Private Smee time precisely 45 minutes from the fuses?

Mexican Standoff

*"Let your rapidity be that of the wind,
your compactness be that of the forest."*

As the sun beats down on a long-forgotten dusty and sandy town square, way, way back somewhere in America's Wild West, three macho gunslingers, with thick mustaches and even bigger egos, stand tall, locked in a standoff. Each of the three *pistoleros* has a firearm outstretched, sweaty and twitchy fingers on triggers. All of the outlaws have a gun aimed at them.

Their names are Petey, a large-bellied man with long legs; Paulie, a tall man with strong arms; and Pokey, a regular-sized Joe (but don't call him that to his face).

Cowardly onlookers peer from saloon door shutters. A horse whinnies in the background. The only shot that can be heard is ol' shoesmith Clint Doonie drinking his noon-time whiskey on his porch.

But this is no ordinary standoff.

Each of the three sharpshooters is out of bullets. They were expended mere moments earlier in the pursuit of each other to this point.

No one knows what to do next.

Just as things start to get awkward, a croaky voice bursts forth from the nearby saloon.

"The nearest munitions store is two miles north."

Each of the cowboys looks at the other.

Petey speaks: "Let's settle this here dispute there then."

Paulie speaks: "I'm good with that if y'all are good with that."

Pokey speaks: "Me too."

And then they run off as quickly as their spurs can jangle.

Petey jumps on his bicycle—a newfangled contraption, but cheaper than a horse.

Paulie jumps on his unicycle; he can't afford a bicycle. Or a horse.

And Pokey runs; he has legs as strong as a horse.

Each of the gunslingers races along a straight path across the dense sandy path all the way to the munitions store.

When this reporter turns up at the scene, all we learn is that Paulie is dead. Everything else is a mystery… so what happened?

Old Enemies

"Pretend to be weak, that your enemy may grow arrogant."

"Mr President, the President will see you now…"

A tall man in a decorated soldier's uniform opens a large oak door and ushers the President of Paraguay, Solano López—an impetuous and uneducated man approaching his 75th year—into a dark, candlelit banquet room. In the corner, a fire rages. Hunched over the fire stands Flores Barrio, the President of Uruguay, slightly older than his lifelong enemy. He is throwing what look like maps, files and plans into the fire.

"For 12 long years, our countries have been at each other's throats, Solano," Barrio whispers. "It's time for it to end, for our children… and their children."

Barrio coughs loudly, a cough that echoes deep and heavy around the empty room.

"It is your war, Flores—brought to my door," Solano replies. "My children!"

Barrio moves away from the fire and moves slowly, unsteadily, toward a large banquet table. His movements are calculated and precise, but slow.

"Sit, Solano, please. Let us talk like men—not bark like nine hungry dogs."

López takes a seat at the opposite end of a long wooden banquet table, his eyes never deviating from his opponent's movements.

Barrio sits on a large, ornate chair, although he seems to collapse into it more than sit, his frail body shadow dancing in the light of the fire.

"You've grown weak," says López. "Is that why you've brought me here—can you no longer stomach the fight? You want a truce? Ha!"

Barrio exhales through his nose and allows a deep, chesty cough to rip through the room.

"No truce, Solano. I want our war to end tonight," croaks Barrio. "My days are numbered. My six children and 11 grandchildren implored me to seek a higher outcome from this war."

"And how do you propose for that to happen?" replies López. "Flip a coin?"

"No," says Barrio. "Don't be ridiculous. But how about a roll of the dice?"

López stands up and his chair squeals loudly as he thrusts it backwards with his legs.

"You must be as crazy as you are old!" López shouts. "You're going to give up your people's future on a roll of the dice? Your mind must be as weak as your body."

"Maybe," Barrio whispers. "I am not as I was once, but I'm still twice the man you are. Are you still a man of your word, Solano?"

"Of course I'm a man of my word—not like your people. I'll beat your foolish game."

López cracks his knuckles.

"Hmm," mumbles Barrio. "Then let us end the suffering of our two families and our people. Why should they die at the hands of two old men who can no longer fight for themselves?"

Barrio places two dice on the banquet table.

López looks at them with disbelief and hunger.

"He who rolls the number they call wins. You can go first."

What is the number López should call in order beat Barrio?

Resistance

"Fighting with a large army under your command is nowise different from fighting with a small one."

In shadows deep, I stealthily tread,
An ambush of whispers where I'm led.
No uniform, no banners fly,
My resistance makes foes wonder why.

With eager eyes, an insurgent's gun,
Asymmetric echoes of a hit and run.
King of jungle's covert throne,
Unconventional domains I call my own.

With mobile steps I slip through night,
A rebellion veiled in darkness' might.
No open fields, no warfare grand,
I am undercover, like shifting sand.

I blend with trees, become the breeze,
A saboteur's game among the leaves.
No fixed abode, a clandestine twist
Unlike my namesake camouflaged in mist.

In whispers soft, my movements are told,
A little war, never bold.
No fame I seek, just freedom's fight,
Who am I, undercover in the night?

War Hero

*"Force your enemy to reveal himself,
so as to find out his vulnerable spots."*

Obituary: General Carlos Hernandez

Born: March 19, 1801   Died: November 7, 1875

General Carlos Hernandez, a revered military figure from 19th-century South America, passed away on November 7, 1875, at the age of 74. Born on March 19, 1801, in the quaint village of San Miguel, he emerged as a visionary leader during a tumultuous era of change and independence.

Hernandez hailed from a family of farmers and artisans, a modest background that instilled in him a deep connection to the struggles of the common people. With an insatiable thirst for knowledge, he defied societal norms and pursued education to its highest form, fostering a passion for history, strategy and literature that would define his legacy. He graduated from the University of Buenos Aires on July 15, 1823.

His illustrious military career was set in motion during the War of Independence in the 1820s. As a young lieutenant, he displayed remarkable tactical prowess during the Battle of Rio Azul, which began on January 13, 1824, a clash that marked the beginning of his meteoric rise. On September 11, 1827, as a seasoned Captain, he devised a daring night ambush that secured a strategic bridge and forced the enemy's retreat, earning him the rank of Major.

General Hernandez's most celebrated achievement unfolded during the first day of the Civil Uprising, August 9, 1845. As a Lieutenant Colonel, he commanded a diverse coalition of forces with disparate loyalties. His masterful strategy led to the pivotal Battle of San Lorenzo, where he united various factions to repel the common threat. This triumph paved the way for a new era of unity and cooperation, and he was promoted to Colonel in recognition of his strategic genius.

On March 17, 1856, as a Brigadier General, he played a key role in the Battle of Valle del Sol, a turning point in the struggle for regional sovereignty. His unwavering leadership on that day ensured a decisive victory, leading to the signing of the Treaty of Solis that secured the region's autonomy. "This is a great day for our peoples—my family and yours!" he said.

Outside the battlefield, General Hernandez was a devoted family man. He married Isabella Martinez on June 12, 1828, and together they raised three children: Alejandro (born October 13, 1829; died May 27, 1852); Lucia (born March 19, 1831); and Mateo (born April 1, 1834). Despite his demanding career, he made it a point to foster a strong family bond, sharing tales of courage, sacrifice and the importance of standing up for justice.

General Carlos Hernandez's legacy as a brilliant strategist, compassionate leader and visionary statesman is etched in the heart of the nation to which he dedicated his life. His influence extended beyond the battlefield, shaping the nation's identity during a time of transformation and uncertainty.

A state funeral will be held on November 15, 1875, at the capital's cathedral, where he will be laid to rest with a full military ceremony. As South America mourns the loss of a true hero, the memory of General Carlos Hernandez will inspire generations to come.

****

November 16, 1875

Mateo Hernandez stood above an old safe in his late father's office in San Miguel. It had been installed in the house in 1831, as a gift from the president. All Mateo knew was that the code contained six digits. His father had once told him, after a few glasses of *aguardiente,* that the code was the best birthday gift a military man could receive. "I go back in time to that moment to remember good times whenever I open that safe," Hernandez Sr. said.

What is the code?

Leadership

"The general is the bulwark of the State;
if the bulwark is complete at all points, the State will be strong;
if the bulwark is defective, the State will be weak."

The great leader made a speech to his troops. Famous for speaking in riddles but motivating the men and women of the army, he came out with a classic that served to distract the troops and also ready them for the impending battle:

"I am neat and round as a circle, worth nothing if I lead; but when I follow a group, I make the strength of them increase tenfold. By myself I'm worth nothing. What am I?"

Can you figure out what the leader was referring to?

Divide and Conquer

"Do not repeat the tactics which have gained you one victory."

Paris, France, 1805

Alone in his large Château de Malmaison, Napoleon Bonaparte, the French Emperor and one of the world's greatest military strategists, looks down at a litany of maps of Russia and Austria, and other charts of the world, as well stacks and stacks of papers and books all dedicated to the greatest warfare strategies in human history, from Khan to Tzu, Barca to Cao, Alexander the Great to Zhuge Liang—and even his arch nemesis, Wellington—and tries to make sense of them all. His mind is awhirl with battle locations and strategies, from pincer movements to artillery barrage, vertical envelopment to scorched earth, ambush and flanking—every battle technique is whizzing around Napoleon's mind alongside locations as far and broad as Aspern-Essling, Leipzig, Waterloo, Wagram, Marengo and Borodino. Which to choose? Where to go? What to do? And, yet, his great logical intellect is so stuffed with facts and figures, he can't concentrate on a single one.

How illogical, he thinks to himself.

Just then, in among the chaos of this command-table detritus, something catches Napoleon's eye. It is a handwritten note.

"If you find yourself lost in battle," it reads, "look within."

The note continues: "I may be old, but I'm never timeless."

The note is, unmistakably, written by one of Napoleon's most trusted generals, Jean-Baptiste Bernadotte; his advice has been incalculable since the start of the empire's wars.

Bernadotte has given Napoleon a clue. The beginning of a game, Napoleon thinks excitedly. At this point, any distractions are welcome for his clogged neurons.

"A-ha!" Napoleon gasps aloud. "I know!"

With that, Napoleon rushes out of the room.

****

For the next hour, the Emperor is entertained by Bernadotte's *chasse au trésor,* a collection of clues scattered around the château. It helps Napoleon focus his divergent mind.

1. I may be old, but I'm never timeless.
2. I make the rain head back to heaven.
3. I shine and divide while you eat.
4. I spout Indian leaves as I brew.
5. I live in a French drawer when you write.
6. I collect dirt covertly underneath your feet.
7. I illuminate your darkness bright.
8. I will write when dipped into.
9. I collect your clothes abroad.
10. I am six strings but not a guitar.

When Napoleon is done collecting the clues, he looks down at the evidence and sees that not only has Bernadotte crafted a most excellent game for Napoleon's amusement, he has also cunningly worked out Napoleon's next battle plan.

It becomes the Emperor's greatest victory.

From Bernadotte's clues, can you figure out Napoleon's next battle move?

A Lucky Find

"The material for raising fire
should always be kept in readiness."

Lost in the desert after the Battle of Abukir, as the sun goes down and the temperature drops Fernand stumbles across a crate that must have been dislodged from a supply cart earlier in the day in the confusion of battle. According to the label, it contains water bottles, bread, a packet of tea, tobacco and matches. What should the cold, thirsty, starving man open first?

Angels and Demons

"The soldier works out his victory in relation to the foe whom he is facing."

Tom Grant and John Tucker were two American prisoners in the Napoleonic wars. They had been imprisoned in Dartmoor Prison, a place the British had constructed for the sole reason of keeping POWs locked away until the end of the conflict.

It had been 380 days since Tom or John had tasted fresh air or walked freely as admirable men.

John could see that his cellmate Tom had begun to fade within himself. He had started to give up hope that he would ever see his wife and children again, or feel the fields beneath his feet back home on American soil. Tom was losing his own internal battle in this godforsaken war.

One day, when Tom appeared particularly retracted and anguished, John decided to try and boost Tom's mood with a brainteaser, a game to divert the mind from its darkest recesses. So he began to tell a story in the hope Tom would engage. He knew if he couldn't keep his, and Tom's, mind from slipping into madness, all hope was lost.

"Back home in New Jersey, when I was a boy," John began, "my father and I used to play a game. I see now it was more of a test than a game, but as a father myself, like you, Tom, every game with your children can be turned into a way to test, push and expand their minds. During one particular game, my father told me all about the significance of the numbers 1-1-1. Apparently, all around the world, these numbers are incredibly important to ancient cultures. They are known as angel numbers, numbers that protect you when you are feeling the most vulnerable and filled with demons. I think we could both use those numbers right now, don't you, Tom?"

John looked up at his friend, but Tom was still lying down on the cold cobblestone floor.

"This game involved summoning these angel numbers from nothing, and my father told me that when I needed to protect what I loved most, I should summon these angel numbers."

Then John, using the sharpest edge of a stone that had worn free of the floor, began to scrape three numbers into the solid stone, one per stone.

It looked like this on the floor:

"Tom," John said, "can you help me summon our angel numbers to help protect us in this demonic prison? The only thing I know is that every row, column and diagonal must add up to 111. When they do, we will be protected by the angels!"

Tom sat up and smiled for the first time in many days. He nodded to his friend and looked at the floor.

"These angels are odd," he said.

Can you fill in the numbers so each row, column and diagonal adds up to 111? And note what is special about the numbers used.

Fool a Fool

"A whole army may be robbed of its spirit;
a commander-in-chief may be robbed
of his presence of mind."

The two commanders met in the field that separated the two armies; Bernard le Fou faced George Toutbon. Le Fou was famed far and wide for his unconventional methods of waging war. But Toutbon was ready—"expect the unexpected," his king had told him—so he was prepared for some form of lunacy from this southern idiot. Or was he?

"Answer me this correctly, and my army and I shall disappear whence we came and leave you in peace. Answer me wrong and you should prepare for a bloody eve." The large man spoke with an accent.

"What is your question?" Toutbon thought it would be something like this—a clever wordplay. He was ready.

Le Fou spoke slowly and clearly: "To prevent this battle, you must name me three consecutive days of the week. But you must not use any of the following: Sunday, Monday, Tuesday, Wednesday, Thursday, Friday or Saturday."

Toutbon swore to himself and racked his brain. He really wanted to avoid a fight, to protect his men and his lord's land.

What should he reply?

Behind Enemy Lines

"Five constant factors:
The Commander."

Commander William Aldridge stood wearily in his command tent on the outskirts of Kabul. Maps and charts of the war-torn region spread before him, treaties fallen to the floor. The conflict had not gone well, and Lord Melbourne, the Prime Minister, was beginning to question Aldridge's strategies. As a response, and to regain control of the Afghan borders, Aldridge had summoned his four most trusted generals to discuss new strategies for the upcoming battle of Ghazni. It was crucial that the British advanced, or at least held, their position.

As the conversation flowed and they discussed battle formations and supply routes, Aldridge drank from a flagon of wine.

Suddenly, Commander Aldridge's voice grew weaker, his head spinning. He tried to focus, but his vision blurred. He was a bright man with a keen sense of intuition. He knew he had been poisoned and so quickly surveyed the room. He knew that his betrayer had to be close. But he didn't know who.

To his right was General Harrington, as handsome as he was commanding, but underneath his good looks was a fiery ambition for the top job. He had risen through the ranks through sheer force of will, garnering the trust of his soldiers. But was his loyalty genuine?

To his left was General Thornton, a striking figure who possessed an uncanny ability to charm even the most unlikeable diplomats. He was the mastermind behind many successful covert operations, but could his cunning extend to darker deeds?

Behind him was General Darcy, who exuded an air of icy determination when it came to winning, and was the first to initiate a strategy. He was a master tactician, cunning and precise, and had always supported the commander's decisions—at least so far.

In front of Aldridge was General Westfield. Of all Aldridge's generals, Westfield was the quietest, his gaze often distant as if deciphering the movements of the stars in his mind. His sharp intellect was perhaps the greatest in the room, yet an indifference lurked beneath his calm disposition. What was he thinking?

"Commander, are you well?" General Thornton asked.

"I... I'm not feeling —" Commander Aldridge's words faltered, his strength abandoning him. He fell to the floor, writhing. As he looked up for the last time, he saw General Darcy, frozen, General Harrington rushing to speak to a soldier at the door, and General Westfield looking panicked.

Who poisoned the commander?

On the Run

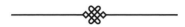

"Do not pursue an enemy who simulates flight."

Fleeing from the Battle of Borodino, Sergei runs as fast and as far as he can from the conflict. He comes across six ragged *Desyatnik*, each with five men. He meets seven tired *Pyatidesyatnik*, each accompanied by four wounded men, and a cook and a dragoon between them. Finally, he meets a *Golova*, along with his personal butler, four men carrying his affairs, and his chef.

How many in total are escaping the battle?

Horseplay

"Hold out baits to entice the enemy."

Stuck in a stalemate after months of fruitless aggression, two generals meet on neutral territory. They cannot agree on a way to settle the original argument. A battle is too bloody. A champion duel too simple. Then one general suggests a race between their two finest riders. Slightly worried by this—despite thinking it's the least bloody possibility—the other agrees, but with one stipulation: the owner of the slower horse will triumph, i.e. a race to come second. The other general ponders this, but likes the twist it can bring, so agrees. However, on the day of the race it all looks dreadful. Moving as slowly as they possibly can, the two riders take hours to cover even the smallest distance; it is insufferable.

Out of the blue, a wizened old man limps up to the riders as they take a short break. After that, the riders leap back onto the horses, but this time at full speed and the race is over swiftly. What did the wise man tell them?

Masterpieces

"There are not more than five primary colors
(blue, yellow, red, white and black), yet in combination
they produce more hues than can ever be seen."

Winston Churchill, the Prime Minister of Great Britain and a keen painter, sat alone in his apartment above Downing Street looking blankly at a lifeless canvas. With a glass of Dom Perignon in one hand and a dry brush in another, Winston was defeated by his own imagination. Needing to create a piece of art after a tiring day of politics, Winston didn't know where to start—or what to paint.

The problem was that each of the paint jars to his left—red, blue, green, yellow, purple—had been incorrectly tagged; it was a creative challenge he'd set himself months before, but now could not recall, or was too tired to remember the answer.

However, he could summon three important facts:

The jar with a tag marked green contained either blue or red paint.
The jar with a tag marked red contained green paint.
The jar with a tag marked blue contained yellow paint.

Taking a sip of Champagne, the great strategic thinker thought out loud. "An optimist sees opportunity in every difficulty."

And then the answer hit him.

How did Winston figure out which shade of paint was in each jar without opening them to look?

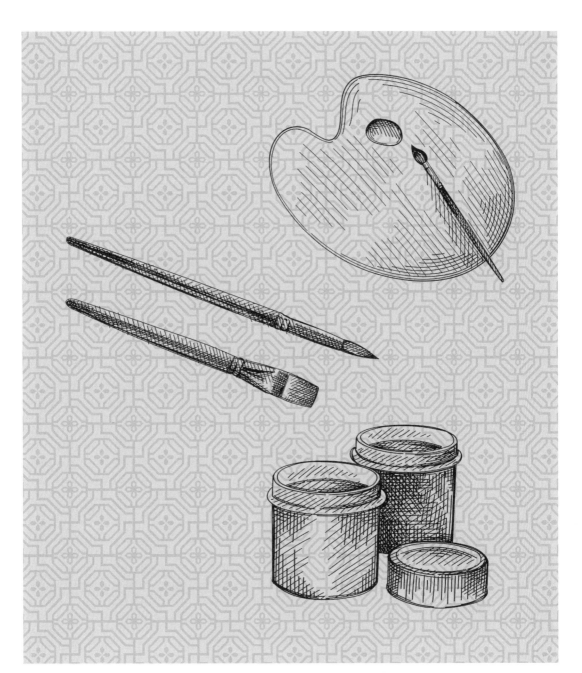

White House Down

"If the enemy leaves a door open, you must rush in."

"Quick, this way, now!" Frank Greer, President Wilson's most trusted bodyguard, shouts back to his Eagle unit, some of whom may now be dead. Greer, carrying the president in his two arms because Eagle has been shot in the leg and is unconscious, aggressively moves forward down a labyrinth of connected hallways at a running pace. Greer, too, has been hit, in the chest, possibly twice. He's losing blood quicker than he can run.

Behind him—following him—a group of hostiles are in quick pursuit, maybe four masked men, maybe more, details unknown. Greer can only assume they have come to take the president hostage. They must fail. Greer's only job is to get the president to safety, locked securely behind the impenetrable steel walls in the White House's underground bunker, within the next 60 seconds, and call for military support. He must succeed.

As Greer reaches the bunker's entrance, he is presented with a security passcode sequence, a keycode that is only enforced when White House security is breached. It changes hourly. All that's missing is a two-digit number.

$$1 - 3 - 7 - 15 - 31 - ?? - 127$$

With the president out cold, Greer will have to figure out the number for himself, before it's too late. What is the number?

Clue: It's the president's age.

Winds of Time

*"Anger may in time change to gladness;
vexation may be succeeded by content."*

Carter pushed into the small gap that had been opened up over the past few days. Callender, the expedition's engineer, had taken two days to install lights for the big reveal. After months of camping out in—admittedly—quite luxurious conditions, the team was ready to go in; a telegram to the king was ready too.

Carter and Callender squeezed through the gap, helping Lord Carnarvon through too. The nobleman's health had deteriorated steadily over the past few months; little did any of them know, but he would be dead in a matter of weeks. The buzz from the lights was the only sound except for the shuffling of feet and the occasional exhalation. A metallic yellow light shone on a series of hieroglyphics in prominent positions on the path. Carter said, "This one must be important—get Ahmed's son." "Sure," replied Callender, walking back to the entrance. It wasn't long before he was back with Ahmed Said's son, one of few fluent ancient Egyptian readers and English speakers. Carnarvon gestured to the beautifully preserved script on the wall: "Well? What does that mean?" The boy, only 14 years old, was terrified of the old gentleman. "I must look, sir, will not take long."

"Well go on, then, read it boy," came the grouchy response.

The boy went as quickly as he could, touching the cold wall as he deciphered the symbols.

"It is… a question, sir. How do you say, a puzzle?"

"A riddle? Is that it?"

"Yes, sir, a riddle. It is a question to answer."

"Well what does it say, then?"

The boy spoke slowly, reading carefully, constructing the sentences beautifully as he translated the text from a language thousands of years old…

"I do not have a past, I only have a future,
But nothing more do I possess,
Only the trust of every man and every woman, from pharaoh to slave."

"What the hell does that mean? Some kind of curse? More bloody mumbo jumbo?" Carnarvon was not a believer.

Callender took a gentler approach. "What do you think it means, young one? Should we be worried?"

What is the answer to the riddle?

Renegades

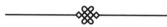

"Bringing anarchy into the army causes victory to be thrown away."

Mikhail Bakunin, a Russian revolutionary and philosopher, and one of the founding fathers of modern anarchism, believed in the abolition of all forms of authority and hierarchy. "The urge to destroy is also a creative urge," he wrote of his passion to introduce pure anarchy into the everyday world, one of his many well-known sayings about standing up to established order.

To celebrate Bakunin always having the right word for an anarchic occasion, we've assembled an anarchy-based word-search grid. How many words can you find?

You may spot something extra anarchic in the grid too; what is it?

```
O B N J G V E E K P A D X K
L H U S R T R G F R W V T E
E O C S E R W E X A S K A N
A T I D T L E U O S O B G G
S N T K T S H F D S O U O V
S G Y T E R W B U X P L V S
I L L R I C J E C W S A G J
T D T P R E R T E R L C R K
A I W E A E O X I R W T M C
D U D U T T W I O H I L E N
Y K T U H C E X B N G E A H
S I O L O F O E H E N S V T
```

Tired Talk

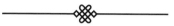

*"Appear at points which the enemy must hasten to defend;
march swiftly to places where you are not expected."*

After a full day's march, sitting beside the fire in the open air on the way to Hardknott Fort, Marius says to Maximus, "Answer me this if you can: The more you take, the more you leave behind. What is it?"

Payout

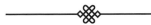

"That there may be advantage from defeating the enemy, men must have their rewards."

After a fruitful raid on enemy positions, it is time for the treasure to be divided up among the raiders, a group of grizzled veterans. They make it back with five bags of gold that all look identical, and each bag contains 10 gold coins. However, after a tip-off from a turncoat, it becomes apparent that one of the five bags is made up of fake gold instead. The real gold, fake gold, and all the bags are identical in every way. The only difference is that the pieces of fake gold each weigh 1.1 grams, against the real gold pieces, which weigh 1 gram each. The group has the use of a very accurate scale, but time is tight, so it can only be used for one weight measurement.

How should the group figure out which bag contains the fake gold?

Load the Wagons

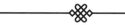

*"The skillful soldier does not raise a second levy,
neither are his supply-wagons loaded more than twice."*

The commander gives his orders: "Exactly half of the carts must be loaded with ammunition and shipped to the front right away—and that means *right away*, soldier." Private Shaw's problem is that there are only three wagons, and he is responsible for loading them up and getting those valuable supplies to the front. He cannot go and reason with the commander; even explaining the situation will take too long. What should Private Shaw do?

Battle of Equals

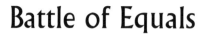

"He will win who knows how to handle both superior and inferior forces."

A general controls his small army against an enemy force that is exactly the same size. When the armies face each other it is almost like looking in a mirror; there are only two small differences. When one general admits defeat, the battlefield is swept clean, the fallen removed as soon as they tumble. One general allows the other to go first, always in the same order; sometimes there is no winner. Which war is this?

Shootin' Talk

*"The good fighters of old first put themselves
beyond the possibility of defeat, and then waited
for an opportunity of defeating the enemy."*

Mr Bueno, Mr Feo, and Mr Malo get caught up in a strange kind of gunfight. They take turns shooting, and the last man standing is the winner. Mr Bueno hits his target 1/3 of the time, Mr Feo hits his target 2/3 of the time and Mr Malo hits his target ALL the time (3/3). You are Mr Bueno, shooting first, after which it is Mr Feo's turn (if he's still alive), then Mr Malo (again, if he's still alive).

Where should you shoot for the best odds of survival? All the shooters know each other's odds.

Supplies

"The good general cultivates his resources."

You are the quartermaster and there's a problem in the supply chain: the Apples, Bananas and Mixed Fruit crates have been mixed up. One crate contains only apples. One contains only bananas and one contains a mixture of the two. The labels Apples, Bananas and Mixed Fruit have all been incorrectly applied. General Zed hates bananas and won't even tolerate a mixture, so you must figure out which crate is which and make sure the apples are delivered to him. You only have time to open one crate before they are shipped off. If it's not the one containing apples, how do you figure out which one contains only apples?

The Bridge

*"In all fighting, the direct method may be used
for joining battle, but indirect methods will be needed
in order to secure victory."*

Lieutenant Smits watches the battle rage from the other side of the river. His side is losing, and he needs to cross over to get into the thick of the action. A mechanical bridge, operated by a simple lever, stands in his way; the bridge is up and uncrossable. He can see the gears—five in all—that are linked to each other. To lower the bridge he needs to figure out if the fifth gear will turn counterclockwise or clockwise as he turns the lever clockwise. Which way will it turn? The handle is attached directly to the first gear.

Capture!

"Energy may be likened to the bending of a crossbow; decision, to the releasing of a trigger."

The battle is over, except for the capturing of the enemy, who are running around the battlefield in disarray. Culky doesn't want them to be harmed, so it's a roundup job. You and five of your soldiers catch six prisoners in six minutes. How many soldiers do you need if you want to catch 60 prisoners in one hour?

Give and Take

"In the wise leader's plans, considerations of advantage and of disadvantage will be blended together."

Three grizzled mercenaries are ready for a fight and have all checked themselves in to the hostelry next to the barracks where they will present themselves the next day, ready to join up for fame and fortune. But mostly fortune.

The innkeeper has charged them 30 groats for the room—10 groats each—so he has 30 groats in his sack. His helpful wife informs him that the room, without board, is 25 groats and that the guests will surely spend more than that on food and drink that night, so he should refund them 5 groats. Realizing he cannot split 5 groats between the 3 of them, he instead gives them 1 groat each and pockets 2 himself—his wife will never notice, after all.

Now the guests have paid a total of 27 groats for the room (30 minus 3) and the innkeeper has 2 groats in his pocket. Where has the other 1 gone?

Bridge Over Troubled Water

"The quality of decision is like the well–timed swoop of a falcon which enables it to strike and destroy its victim."

Routed after a battle, four bedraggled soldiers are fleeing back home. Journeying at night in the driving rain, they come across a rickety bridge that is their only way back. The floodwater is rising and the rain pours down. They have one torch between them and it is essential for safe crossing. There is no time to delay; the decision of who to cross, and when, must be made immediately.

Jacquouille can cross the bridge in 2 minutes
Édouard, who is injured, takes 10 minutes
Frénégonde takes 5 minutes
Godefroy takes 3 minutes

What is the shortest time in which they can all get safely across the bridge?

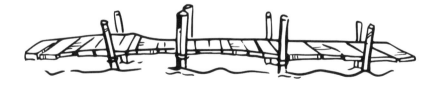

Coded Message

"The second best form of generalship is to prevent the junction of the enemy's forces."

The general has been waiting impatiently for word from his most important spy, who has been working deep between enemy lines for days. The spy is in charge of finding out what would be the best time for the big push forward. Suddenly, a bang at the door reveals a guard. In his hand is a piece of paper that has been shot across the river on an arrow, no doubt by the spy. It contains the following encoded message:

All through the alleys come knights, never over water.

Confused by this cryptic message, the general sends for his best codebreaker. He works it out in seconds. What does the general do, and why?

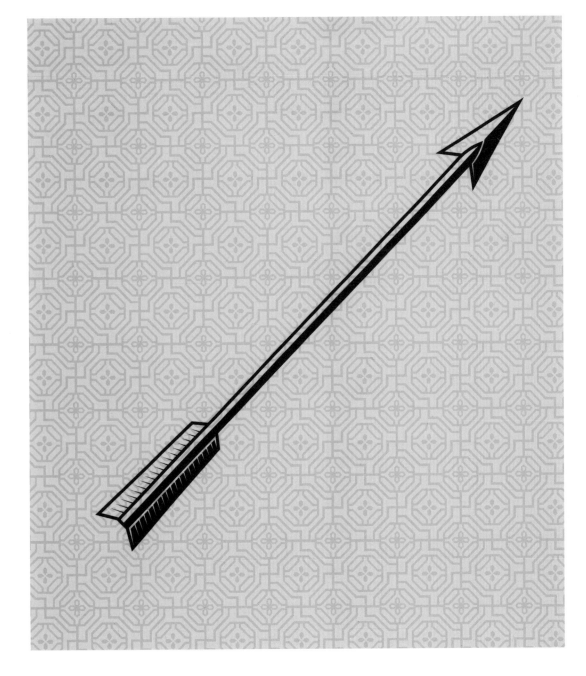

Long Division

"It is the rule in war, if our forces are ten to the enemy's one, to surround him; if five to one, to attack him; if twice as numerous, to divide our army into two."

When planning the attack, General Alcazar has found a way of letting his generals know how many troops to deploy—always more than the enemy. He writes them down in a code, as shown in the box below. Which numbers should replace the question marks in the grid, and what is the logical sequence it is part of?

?	3	10
?	4	10
?	2	7
?	6	10
?	6	9
?	3	?

Barents Sea

Norwegian Sea

North Atlantic Ocean

Finland

Norway

Sweden

Gulf of
Bothnia

St. Petersburg

Clyde   Edinburgh

North Sea

Skagerrack

Denmark

Liverpool

Yorkshire

Wales   London

Heligoland
Bight

Baltic Sea

Livonia

Moscow

Irish Sea

English Channel

Holland

Kiel

Berlin

Prussia

Belgium

Ruhr

Silesia

Warsaw

Picardy

Ukraine

Sevastopol

Brest

Munich

Bohemia

Galicia

Mid-Atlantic Ocean

Paris

Burgandy

Tyrolia

Vienna

Gascony

Marseilles

Piedmont

Budapest

Venice

Trieste

Portugal

Tuscany

Adriatic Sea

Rumania

Black Sea

Spain

Gulf of Lyons

Rome

Apulia

Serbia

Bulgaria

Armenia

Western Mediterranean

Tyrrhenian Sea

Naples

Albania

Greece

Ankara

Smyrna

Aegean
Sea

Constantinople

North Africa

Tunis

Ionian Sea

Eastern Mediterranean

Syria

Adding Up

*"If quite unequal in every way,
we can flee from an enemy."*

Coded messages from spies were essential before, during and after a battle. The general's best spy has sent the following coded message:

1, 4, 5, 6, 7, 9, 11, ?

The general wants to know the number of divisions that are waiting in the port he plans to attack. To cover up the number, the spy has written a simple sequence. If the general can figure out what comes next, he will know the number. What is it, and why?

An Odd Number

*"The opportunity of defeating the enemy
is provided by the enemy himself."*

December 18, 1945

Albert Einstein slowly opened the heavy wooden door to a Princeton lecture hall. As he approached the table at the front of the class, he placed his brown leather case on top and took a long, deep and lingering look at the clock at the back of the room. He inhaled through his nose, and breathed out through his mouth, a sigh that seemed to echo around the lecture hall. There was a weight to Einstein's movement, a mass, if you will. Each action was heavy and gentle, as if it bent time in slow motion. He made a meal of squinting to see the time, which made the throng of 50 or so students laugh—no mean feat considering the gravity of the atomic events earlier in the year.

On the blackboard behind Einstein were the words "On the Generalized Theory of Gravitation," written in chalk by one of his assistants before the lecture; it was meant to be the theme of today's cosmological lecture. Instead of starting to talk, as is customary in these situations, Einstein was in one of his humorous moods, as he often was, and simply lifted up the cuff of his jacket and wiped the words out, much to the audible surprise of his students. He then grabbed a piece of chalk, showed the chalk to the class, and began to mark on the blackboard:

151

"Strive not to be a success, but rather to be of *value*," Einstein then stressed. He picked up his bag and waved goodbye to the students in his famously German way. And then he walked out of the room.

"That's odd," said a student.

"That's Einstein," said another.

What was Einstein trying to say?

Decision Time

*"You can be sure of succeeding in your attacks
if you only attack places which are undefended."*

The decision has come to attack the enemy. A spy has sent the coded message; each number refers to an enemy position and the number of battalions surrounding it:

Zero – 2 battalions
One – 2 battalions
Three – 2 battalions
Five – 2 battalions
Six – ?

"We'll attack Camp Six," the general says, and he is right. Why?

Extraction

"Throw your soldiers into positions whence there is no escape, and they will prefer death to flight."

You are a spy. Your name is of no importance. You're being held hostage at a heavily guarded facility. It doesn't matter where. A unit of allied soldiers is outside the compound. They are here to extract you. However, the enemy has been alerted to their presence. They can no longer come to you. You have to get to them.

You must navigate a series of hallways while avoiding security patrols. All you have is a map that was handed to you by a security guard who was paid off by the extraction team while off duty. You now have to run for your life. Which path will you take?

Extraction point

You are here.

Death by...?

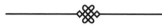

"The experienced soldier, once in motion,
is never bewildered."

Successful businessman and part-time reservist for the National Guard Gerald Grant was found with a package next to him in a field in Arkansas by a farmer on his morning walk. Gerald had many boardroom enemies, and was found on a small island in the middle of a small lake. There were no footprints on the very muddy island, no weapons and no signs of foul play. The police were called but, after a five-minute inspection and a call to the local army base the sheriff declared that he knew the cause of death and also that no further action need be taken.

How did Gerald die?

Self-Destruct

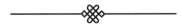

"He will win who knows when to fight and when not to fight."

CIA Agent Luke Ellis stands at the entrance of a top-secret nuclear facility known as The Sphere. His mission is to find a transponder at the heart of the building and simply switch the device off with the touch of a button. To do so ensures that his 10-strong unit of soldiers, waiting on the periphery of the facility's grounds, will be able to evacuate the area safely without being tracked by satellite. It's no easy feat; it's a building designed to keep intruders going around in circles. Ellis needs to make it in or his team won't make it out.

To make matters more interesting, Ellis has just 120 seconds to reach the middle before the enemy encroaches upon his unit's presence and they're all dead.

Can you figure out Ellis's route to the middle in time?

Warning

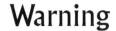

"To hear the noise of thunder is no sign of a quick ear."

Two fathers were walking in the forest with their sons. There was a rumble of thunder and, back at base camp, Sister Davina heard the following:

"Thunder!"
"Thunder!"
"Thunder!"

Each man and son called out once only. None had lost their voices and each was audible outside the forest. How could this happen?

Plans

"The highest form of generalship is to balk the enemy's plans."

Three prisoners have been captured: Archie, Ben and Charles. Ben has with him a copy of the enemy's plans, but the others have false plans, planted as a ruse. However, the interrogator knows the following: Archie always tells the truth and Ben and Charles always lie. How does he figure out which one is Ben, and therefore who has the real plans?

Crossy Road

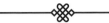

*"All armies prefer high ground to low,
and sunny places to dark."*

Zeke is on his way to a meeting downtown. He's out of the subway and about to cross the road when he sees a woman in the middle of the road and a black truck heading toward her. She's all dressed in black. The streetlights are off. The truck's headlights are not on. Zeke is about to scream—he's too far away to help in any way—when the truck puts on its brakes and the woman carries on and crosses the road; crisis averted. How did the truck driver notice the woman?

Psychological Warfare

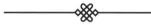

*"In war, the way is to avoid what is strong
and to strike at what is weak."*

Arnold Petraeus, a socially awkward Harvard University professor with an IQ of 164, and an EQ much lower, bites into his lunchtime sandwich, a chicken club with fries and a side salad. As he eats, he reads a biography of Arthur Wellesley—apt, perhaps, as the professor of Conflict and Negotiation and War and Statecraft at the university.

As he wipes the side of his mouth clean, a student he knows as Roland Hall positions himself in parallel to Petraeus's table as if to strike in a pincer movement. Petraeus repositions himself, ready to break Hall's lines and counterattack.

"Sir," Hall starts. "What do you think is the greatest military strategy in the whole of human history?"

Petraeus scoffs. "That's easy."

"What is it?" Hall responds, hoping for an easy answer.

Petraeus, realizing the importance of psychological warfare at the heart of all conflicts, starts to write down a stream of numbers in a seemingly never-ending sequence:

1 14 1 18 13 25 13 1 18 3 8 5 19 15 14 9 20 19 19 20 15 131 3 8

"Napoleon was skilled at adapting his tactics to the evolving situation on the battlefield," Petraeus begins. "He was known to make decisions quickly based on the changing circumstances, which often caught his enemies off guard. I suggest you work it out yourself, Hall."

With that, Petraeus takes a bite of his sandwich and retreats into his book.

What is the answer to Hall's question?

Agent of Chaos

"Be subtle! Be subtle!
And use your spies for every kind of business."

A government agency—we won't say which one—suspects that a known foreign terrorist organization is about to detonate a bomb at a particular landmark in a major European city. They've picked up an FM radio channel looping the same message. The agency believes it is the destination and time where a bomb will explode today.

This is the clue:

Iron bones, steadfast and true… 10… 2… 3… 10… 2… 3. A monument where moments begin… History and present intertwine, brassy hue… 10… 2… 3… 10… 2… 3. A tower's watchman and city's soul… A legacy etched in a sentinel's tail… 10… 2… 3… 10… 2… 3.

Where on earth could it be and at what time?

Boardroom Bravado

"A victorious army opposed to a routed one, is as a pound's weight placed in the scale against a single grain."

Brad and Jake are always at each other's throats. In the boardroom, on the trading floor, in the bar. Constantly trying to outdo the other has become expected, and neither likes to disappoint. Brad's numbers are through the roof this month, though, so Jake will have to dig deep to come up with a way to get one over on his colleague. After a few beers in JJ Foley's, he has an idea, and offers the following challenge to Brad: "Hey Brad, I've got a superpower. It's that I can tell *exactly* how much someone weighs just by looking at them. I'm the only one with the power... want to test me?"

Brad can't resist, plus he's been working out lately so he's heavy for his size—packing plenty of muscle, as he tells himself each morning. "Sure thing, Jake, let's make it interesting, though. Say, 100 bucks?"

Jake can't believe his luck, and jumps on it. "You bet, let's go. Now, to be clear, if I write your precise weight on this piece of paper, you lose the bet and you give me the money, right?"

Brad smiles as he nods in agreement. "Sure."

Jake takes a long look at his colleague, then scribbles on a piece of paper and folds it once. He passes it to Brad.

Brad's smile drops as he picks up the paper and opens it.

He places a 100-dollar bill on the table and walks out without a word.

What is written on the paper?

Infinite Alternate

*"Numerical weakness comes from
having to prepare against possible attacks."*

Every year while he was alive, world-famous computer technology pioneer, mathematical genius and consummate prankster Stephen Bridge, and fellow genius-cum-nemesis Dominic Miles, would send each other dizzyingly difficult IQ, logic and brain-teaser puzzles to solve on their birthdays. If a puzzle went unsolved, the recipient had to either donate to charity or agree to an extreme physical dare. Both men had fierce intelligence but admitted they lacked the EQ to handle "feelings."

For more than two decades their tech-data companies competed for market share and growth with an ever-increasing competitiveness until both were nearly as global as the other. Today, both companies are valued at more than 1 trillion US dollars.

Earlier this year, Stephen Bridge died suddenly, leaving him unable to say goodbye. However, in the event of his sudden passing, Bridge was prepared. The day after he died, Bridge's email account sent Miles a web link to a fake, and humorous, online news-agency obituary outlining Bridge's life and death. Miles laughed when he read it. However, in the small print underneath the obituary lay a key.

If used, it would unlock Bridge's last prank… and a most revealing personal truth.

Obituary: Stephen Bridge

Born: September 17, 1948   Died: August 2, 2023

It is with heavy hearts (and a kernel panic error that we announce the passing of Stephen Bridge! A brilliant computer and technology pioneer whose legacy is etched in the lines= of code he wrote and the circuits he soldered. With a keyboard in one hand and a soldering iron in the other, he led a life that can only be described as "byte"-sized but monumental. +

{Stephen was born to a family of math enthusiasts, which explains his uncanny ability to count in binary since he was practically a 01. His: fascination with computers began when he managed to dismantle the family's computer and put it back together before anyone even noticed. *He was indeed a prodigy, as long as there was no Ikea furniture involved.

(His ground-breaking achievements in the tech world include inventing a computer mouse with a built-in cheese grater, because why not combine office work and snacking? He also single-handedly solved the problem of tangled cables by introducing the "knot theory+" where you just let the cables do their thing and pretend it's modern art.

Stephen had & unique wit that often had his colleagues in stitches,. His famous line, "I don't always test my code, but when I do, I do it in production, (" became a motto for software developers: worldwide who have ever sprinted towards a rapidly approaching deadline. *

Despite his numerous accomplishments, {he

maintained his humility and often quipped that he was just "a regular guy who happened to be fluent in a few programming languages." His ability to troubleshoot life's problems extended beyond computers; he once fixed a leaky faucet using nothing but a "rubber duck and a couple of lines of Python.

In his free time Stephen enjoyed playing "spot the syntax :/ error" in movies and was an avid collector of vintage floppy disks. He also had a soft spot for retro technology, much to the chagrin of his friends who tried to introduce him to the latest gadgets. {Who needs a smartphone when you have a trusty fax machine, right?

Stephen is survived by his loyal pet dogbot, Sparky, who will require debugging and deworming in Stephen's absence. In lieu of flowers, the Bridge family requests that you CtrlAltDelete any negative thoughts and remember Stephen for the laughter and innovation he brought to our digital lives. "

Rest in peace, Stephen Bridge. May your code compile smoothly in the afterlife and may your Wi-Fi signal always be strong.

! = A   @ = B   # = C $ = D   % = E   ^ = F   & = G   * = H   (= I   ) = J   - = K   _ = L   = M   + = N   { = O

} = P   [= Q   ] = R   ; = S   : = T   " = U   ' = V   , = W   . = X   / = Y   < = Z

Knock Knock

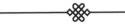

"We cannot enter into alliances until we are acquainted with the designs of our neighbors."

Captain Jellicoe was settling into his new quarters, safely back from the front lines, when there was a knock at the door. He stood up and answered. There stood a young man in uniform. "Oh, I'm sorry," he said, "I thought this was my room—221." "No, it's mine I'm afraid, I've not long been here." The man turned and left, but right away Jellicoe called the military police and told them to question the man. It turned out he was an impostor and thief looking for places to steal from. How did he know?

Hope Springs

*"Water shapes its course according to the
nature of the ground over which it flows."*

Miles and miles of desert sand stretch before Dusty, who has eyes as dry as a bone.
"I need water," he croaks to no one for the 250th time in the last three days. Raging
thirst has left Dusty delirious. All of a sudden, Dusty's eyes well up. "Water!" he
exclaims. "Glorious water!" Everything is going to be alright, Dusty thinks, licking
his dry, cracked lips; Dusty dies less than an hour later.

Why? And how do you know?

Squabbling Siblings

*"The skillful fighter puts himself into a position
which makes defeat impossible, and does not
miss the moment for defeating the enemy."*

Jackson, CFO of Bitter, the social media giant, has the misfortune of bringing both his kids in on "bring your kids to work day." His boss, the eccentric billionaire Kreighton Dust, thinks it's a great idea: "Family bonding is, like, sooo important to the enduring fabric of civilized society." The children argue all day since the Wi-Fi is disconnected and they have to talk to each other instead. Soon it descends into chaos and fisticuffs. Jackson needs to calm his kids down, but he has no idea what to do when the electronics are out. Then he has a brainwave—analogue style. Taking a piece of paper, he says, "You guys both have to stand on this piece of paper and not touch each other." "Yeah, right," snort the kids, ready for another round. But when they are both on the paper it turns out their dad is right, and despite their best efforts, they can't touch each other. Why is this?

Heads or Tails

"That general is skillful in attack whose opponent does not know what to defend."

You are defending four outposts. Each one has a light on the front—either off or on. From your control room you want to turn all of them on, to show the enemy that all outposts are defended (they won't know if there's actually anyone in there or not). Unfortunately, there's a fault in the wiring and you have to activate three switches at the same time, every time. Fortunately, you can choose the switches. How many moves do you have to make in order to flip the switches to get all the lights on?

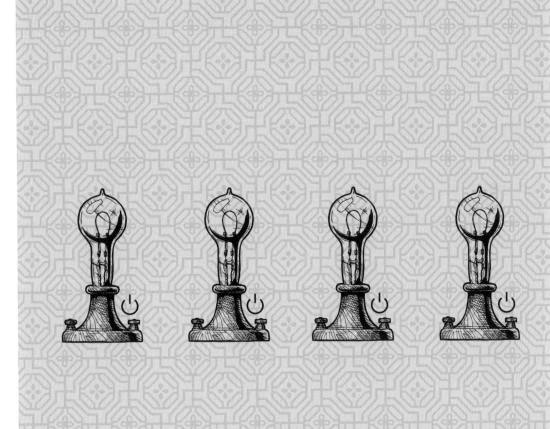

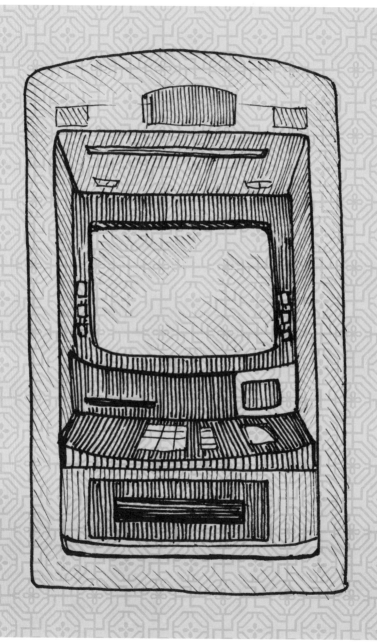

Pull the PIN

*"The onrush of a conquering force is
like the bursting of pent-up waters into
a chasm a thousand fathoms deep."*

Malcolm Croft stands before an ATM. He is standing, frozen, unable to remember the PIN number for his bank card. Without the number, Croft will be unable to buy his family the ice cream he promised them and all hell will break loose; his kids are an unruly lot when they *are* given what they want. When they are denied, there are almost no limits to their naughtiness. Croft stands frozen, but then remembers the memory riddle he devised to ensure he could always remember the PIN.

I am a number between 3,000 and 4,000.
My first digit is one-third of my second digit.
My third digit starts the sum of my first and second digits.
My fourth digit is twice my third digit.

What is Croft's PIN?

Catch and Release

"It is better to recapture an army entire than to destroy it."

Colonel Morales's vehicle, a Range Rover Discovery with blacked-out windows, emerges from the 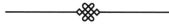 embassy underground parking lot. The congested streets have a new car to contend with. The vehicle's destination is unknown. Onboard contents and personnel are all that have been verified. Morales has been atop the embassy's host nation's Red Notice "Capture" list for the best part of a decade. This is their one chance to seize the day and grab Morales in daylight before he goes underground again.

Intelligence units are in place performing surveillance from the top of surrounding buildings as well as in several tracking vehicles staying close enough behind to ensure they are not spotted as a tail. It's imperative Morales doesn't change his directions—or plans.

"Suspected package in transit," Captain Roberts, located at HQ's bank of monitors, announces over the squawk box. "All eyes on."

A round of "Copy that" echoes around Roberts's FM frequency.

"Can I get a confirmation on the vehicle registration?" Roberts asks the A-Team leader following behind Morales. "Tanner?"

Tanner doesn't reply.

"Tanner?" barks Roberts once.

No reply.

"Tanner!" Roberts barks again.

No reply.

"Tanner!" barks Roberts; the third time's a charm. "Tell me you got the registration!"

"Sort of, sir," Tanner responds statically, then slowly reads out what she sees in her mind's eye. "D... L... Y... 8... 0... R... E... But, remember, I have dyslexia and dyscalculia—the registration is all backwards and binary to me in places—can you help me figure it out?"

Morales evades captured.

What is the actual registration number of Morales's vehicle? And what is Morales's nationality?

Must. Do. It.

"The Commander:
one of the five constant factors."

Jim has a problem. He has fallen under the control of what he calls his commander. The commander can appear at any moment, and Jim feels obliged to obey him. The commander orders him into action—always the same action—and Jim complies. The commander visits other people too, but never speaks his orders. Jim tries to ignore the commander, but he usually can't. When he does what the commander asks, the commander is quiet. For a while… What is the commander?

Drink Up!

*"A wise general makes a point
of foraging on the enemy."*

Stephen, Helen and Dee are drinking coffee.
Sam, David and Simon are drinking tea.
Henryk, Jude and Edith are drinking water.

Judging by his name, what will Peter drink?

EHKLQG WKLV GRRU NLQJGRP

FRPH DZDLWV . XQOHVV BRX QRWLFHG

WKH WULS ZLUH

The Enigma

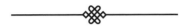

"Divine art of subtlety and secrecy!"

05:00
Location coordinates: ██████████████

A team of three SAS soldiers stealthily approaches the enemy's compound from the west, emerging from a treeline. On schedule. Green light to engage.

A handwritten sign on the compound's door confounds Colonel Arnett, the unit's leader.

Is it a warning?

It's not a language he recognizes.

Arnett instructs his team to fall back to position Delta while he calculates his next move.

EHKLQG WKLV GRRU NLQJGRP
FRPH DZDLWV. XQOHVV BRX QRWLFHG
WKH WULS ZLUH

Why has Arnett asked his unit to fall back?

All-seeing Eye

"In war, the general receives his commands from the sovereign."

On his way to the airport, Grant is in a taxi with his son, who is having some minor discipline trouble at school. As they drive through the crowded city, Grant sets him the following riddle: "I have three eyes. I stare at you. I blink. Sometimes I break. I command you and you obey. What am I?"

How should his son answer?

New Blood

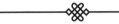

*"To lift an autumn leaf
is no sign of great strength."*

Billionaire CEO and self-proclaimed genius Frederick Reynolds, dressed in a Tom Ford suit worth a small fortune, paces around his large corner office on the 117th floor of the Vanderbilt building, a room encased in tall and thick panes of glass, and looks out across New York's Central Park. His office has perhaps the most sought-after view in all the city. Reynolds places his left hand on the window and sucks air through his teeth, as if literally taking in this breathtaking landscape.

"I'm sick of all these Yes Men, Joe," Reynolds says to his assistant. "Leeches and vampires!"

Reynolds turns around and looks down at a large wooden table and the 12 sullen—scared—faces looking back at him. "Doing something simple doesn't impress me. Get out—all of you!"

At once, the 12 seated figures jolt up and bolt for the door, collecting their laptops as they leave.

Reynolds surveys the landscape outside the window once again. "It's a war out there, you know, Joe. I need more generals—not foot soldiers."

Joe nods in agreement as he closes the door behind his 12 anguished colleagues. "Yes, sir," he responds meekly. He goes to grab his boss a strong coffee… but is interrupted.

"Time for new blood," Reynolds says loudly at the window, as if speaking to the city's citizens below. With that, Reynolds storms out of the room. Joe follows.

Reynolds gallops across the open-plan office floor toward the elevator. There, he presses the down button.

"Down?" says Joe, surprised. "Are we leaving—shall I call the car?"

"No," Reynolds says firmly.

Seconds later, the elevator door opens and Reynolds ushers Joe in. Inside, Reynolds presses the lowest button on the panel, marked B.

The ride down is awkward for Joe. He's never been to the basement level before. He's genuinely scared. The basement is where the non-corporate employees work, blue-collar workers: the mailman, the janitors, the assistants'-assistants'-assistants, the couriers.

After an almost two-minute descent, the elevator door opens and a whole new landscape unveils itself to Reynolds's and Joe's eyes. There are no tall ceilings or thick panes of glass. There are no windows at all. Or spectacular views of Central Park. It is dark, cramped and dingy.

Reynolds storms out of the

elevator toward a whiteboard in the corner. The board is filled with names and numbers, delegations and duties to be completed. Reynolds wipes them out with his tie. His $750 tie. Joe can see Reynolds means business.

Reynolds grabs a black marker and begins to write. Everyone in the basement, more than 30 people, all stand and stare in disbelief that Reynolds—an international celebrity and their company's founder—is here. And communicating with them.

Once Reynolds finishes writing, he turns around and addresses the assembled throng.

"Can you solve this?" he asks, pointing his finger at the person nearest him. The figure looks at the board and gives Reynolds a look of deep I-don't-know.

Reynolds looks at his scribble, and then writes CAN YOU SOLVE THIS? above it.

"Anyone who's brave enough to tell me the correct answer has a job waiting for them on the 117th floor, working directly for me," Reynolds says. With that, he storms back toward Joe and the elevator. And then he vanishes upward. The 30 or so staff gather around the whiteboard and begin to whisper excitedly. "That's easy!" says a courier. "I think."

The board reads:

CAN YOU SOLVE THIS?

$$ \_ + \_ = 30 $$

Fill the spaces with the numbers 1, 3, 5, 7, 9, 11, 13, 15. Repeat the numbers if you want.

Detonation Sequence

"Security against defeat implies defensive tactics; ability to defeat the enemy means taking the offensive."

In five minutes, a war will begin with the detonation of a bomb. The powers that be will be left with no choice but to respond in kind, with likely catastrophic results.

At the bomb's command facility, 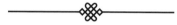 in ▆▆▆▆▆▆▆ (redacted for your safety) a talented physicist named Nicholas Peters is frantically trying to convince military officials to deescalate the situation back to neutral positions. He fails. Diplomacy is dead.

A go-for-launch sequence is initiated.

Sirens blare.

The facility is on lockdown.

In all the confusion and noise, Nicholas forgot that the facility's director, his mysterious mentor, a physicist called Wolf, had secretly built a back-door failsafe code to stop the flight avionics of the bomb's deployment drone. It is Nicholas' last chance to stop the madness.

Nicholas runs up several flights of stairs to the top of the facility to where the drone's launch pad is located. He opens the drone's computer touchscreen terminal and swipes his security ID. Nicholas is then presented with drop-down menu of options. In the bottom right corner, a button flashes DATA-DATA-DATA. He remembered that Wolf had a Sherlock Holmes obsession—a battered old paperback was always in his desk drawer—so Nicholas pressed the button. Could this be Wolf's little joke? Nicholas believed so.

A new screen appeared, with the following sequence of words and crosses:

DATA
XXXX
XXXX
XXXX
XXXX
XXXX
XXXX
XXXX
XXXX
XXXX
XXXX
ATOM

It looks like Wolf's failsafe code. But what does it all mean? Nicholas is stumped. He looks at his wristwatch. He has 90 seconds to stop the end of the world. He has to think fast. But he knows if he gets it right, he could stop the drone from delivering its destruction. Time is running out…

Can Nicholas solve the code sequence?

Bravo Three Echo

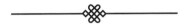

"The Commander stands for the virtue of: courage."

A group of unknown origin, armed with weapons, has taken an unknown number of staff hostage at a government building. They are demanding the release of one of their comrades, currently imprisoned in an international maximum-security facility.

The Prime Minister has ordered her elite military teams to end the siege immediately, and as quietly as possible. The PM, and a team of military and political advisors, stand nervously in a secure location listening in real-time to the operation.

"This is Bravo Three Echo… Bravo Three Echo," the message from Commander Smith, leader of the squad, squawks over the makeshift comms unit. "We're on site, positioned at the rear door. We await authorization to proceed."

"Bravo Three Echo—please confirm visuals on the assailants. How many are there?" asks the PM, fidgety. This is her first hostage situation.

No response.

"Bravo Three Echo, respond. Confirm visual."

No response.

"If they go quiet, it usually means, they cannot speak, ma'am—for fear of giving away their position," says an advisor.

The PM nods, embarrassed.

"Bravo Three—you're authorized to engage immediately," commands the PM out of nowhere.

Silence.

Loud crackling ear-piercing gunfire is suddenly heard over the comms.

A flash-bang explodes.

"There are two assailants in front… of an assailant," jitters Commander Smith's garbled and adrenalin-charged reply, amidst a barrage of noise. "Two assailants behind an assailant… and an assailant in the middle."

The PM looks at her team with a quizzical look.

Ten seconds ticks by.

"Bravo Three Echo. Update?" asks the PM.

"All assailants are down. Eleven hostages safe," Commander Smith responds.

The PM breathes a sigh of relief. "Smith… how many assailants were there?"

Numerical Advantage

*"Though an obstinate fight may be made by a small force,
in the end it must be captured by the larger force."*

Presiding over a big boardroom takeover is not an easy process. You've got to look at all the angles, be ready for any eventuality and push it through when others may be wobbling. Chas is looking at the projected growth pattern of a rival his company is thinking of purchasing. The month-on-month numbers are as follows:

2, 5, 26, 677

He can't believe that this follows a logical pattern, but after a few moments of reflection, he gets it. What is the pattern?

As a bonus, what is the next number?

Wargames

"It is the nature of a log or stone to remain motionless on level ground, and to move when on a slope."

Jonas Blunt, a 13-year-old student from Pasadena, California, is waiting for the munitions store to load. He's out of ammo and weapons after playing a particularly tough three-hour battle in *Battle Cry: First Blood III*, the online modern-warfare tactics and first-person-shooter computer game. In the store, Jonas will convert real-life dollars into online tokens so that he can buy his chosen selection of weapons, ammunition, medic packs and other helpful in-game accessories. Sadly, Jonas's parents have only given him $15, so he must spend the money wisely if he is to succeed in the next online battle.

This is what *Battle Cry: First Blood III*'s munitions store sells:

AK47 & Flamethrower $7
Rocket Launcher & Glock 26 $6
Medic Pack & 60-Second Shield $2
Silencer & Flamethrower $5
Hand Grenade & Medic Pack $4
60-Second Shield & Silencer $3
Glock 26 & Medic Pack $5

At the munitions store, you can mix and match. To do so, players must figure out the individual value of each item.

Can you find out the price of each weapon separately if you know that the prices are not in fractions, and are in increments of a full dollar?

Expending Energy

"The energy developed by good fighting men is as the momentum of a round stone rolled down a mountain thousands of feet in height."

Don is a lunchtime jogger. His colleagues sometimes mock him about this, but he doesn't mind. After all, he's the healthy one. One day after he's been out running, one of his colleagues challenges him to answer the following question:

"Hey, Don, there's a special type of running that leads to a walk; do you know what it is? And no, it's not running so fast that you are exhausted!"

Do you know?

On My Mind

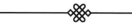

"Moral Law: one of the five constant factors."

Unscrewing a bottle of whiskey as he stands up behind his desk, Chris laughs to himself. It's been a big, busy day but he's made it through—thriving, not just surviving, he says to himself. As a public prosecutor, he has a tough job and he deserves to unwind at the end of a day. One thing is bothering him, though. At lunch with Judge Rhinberg, the senior man asked him a riddle and, not wanting to draw attention to the fact that he couldn't answer it, he moved on as quickly as he could. But it's been bugging him all the rest of the day... The judge said simply:

"You do not want to have it,
But when you do have it,
You do not want to lose it."

What could it be?

Giving and Receiving

"The Commander stands for the virtue of benevolence."

Roving the country from end to end, Gilbert the politician is crossing the land in the hope of raising funds for another campaign, which could prove profitable for the right people. On his way, he stops at six offices in six different towns, and to oil the wheels of industry he takes a sweet donation with him in the form of cakes. To keep the people smiling, at each town he donates half of his cakes, but is always given back a single cake in return. In order to reach his destination with two cakes (one for him, one for the president), how many cakes does Gilbert need to start with?

When the Wind Blows

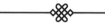

*"Indirect tactics, efficiently applied,
are inexhaustible as Heaven and Earth."*

Trapped on an island, Gabriel is in trouble. He's been sent out to guard the island and to watch out for the invaders. But after a long, hot summer, he's in big trouble. The heavily forested island has started burning—a wildfire set off from the western tip of the island is engulfing everything in its way. The high wind blowing west to east ensures the entire island will be consumed. Gabriel is in the middle and can feel the heat rapidly sweeping toward him. Behind him is only more forest, dry and ready to burn. He cannot leap into the shark-infested water because he cannot swim. He has no tools to dig a trench, and there is no shelter. How does he escape a fiery death?

Simple Sequence

*"The control of a large force is the same principle
as the control of a few men: it is merely
a question of dividing up their numbers."*

What comes next in this sequence?

1
11
21
1211
111221
312211

Held Hostage

"Rapidity is the essence of war:
take advantage of the enemy's unreadiness."

Quick. Answer this and I'll untie you.

It is there once in each and every minute.
But you can only see it once in a millennium.
And then you won't see it in a million years.

What is it?

Flight Not Fight

*"Keep your army continually on the move,
and devise unfathomable plans."*

Two jets take off at exactly the same time. There is only one runway, but there are no crashes, and it is at the same airport. A plane takes more than one minute to take off. How can this happen?

Short Cut to Success

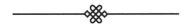

"The enlightened ruler lays his plans well ahead."

Your CEO corners you in the elevator one day. "I like your haircut. Where do you get it done?" You gulp, swallow and lie: "At the barber on River Road, he's the best." You can't risk telling your boss that your mother still cuts your hair. "River Road barbers, you say? There are two on River, the one with the badly cut, messy hair and the one with the really nicely cut, neat hair. Which do you say is the best?"

What do you say, and why?

The Elite Squad

"A soldier's spirit is keenest in the morning."

Captain Daniel Jones has been tasked with assembling an elite group of mercenaries, once distinguished and highly ranked soldiers in the US military for a crucial mission of the utmost importance. The operation is as yet unknown. All that is known at this stage is that Jones must enlist four field-trained members, each famed for their skillset: sniper, demolition, reconnaissance, and medic.

Due to the operation's specialism, and quick deployment, Jones chooses his elite squad, soldiers of fortune he has worked with before, all able to work one other specialization if necessary.

1. Felix Petrov – Sniper

2. Beatrix Long – Demolition

3. Steve Trent – Reconnaissance

4. Bear White – Medic

However, for this covert mission, there's a catch: following enemy intel received, Jones is forced to reassign each soldier to a new role. There are, however, a few unbreakable rules for operational strategy – and success. The rules are as follows:

➤ The sniper can't work demolition due to a previous "explosive incident".

➤ The reconnaissance specialist can only work with viewing instruments.

➤ The sniper must be assigned to a task requiring steady hands and precision.

➤ The reconnaissance specialist can't be assigned to demolition either.

➤ The demolition expert and the sniper both excel in high-pressure situations.

Based on these rules, how should Jones determine which soldier should be reassigned to each task?

Across the river

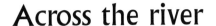

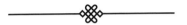

"After crossing a river,
you should get far away from it."

"We need to get out of here!" Myers screams at Nathaniels, his face covered in blood and dust, his rifle empty of all bullets now for several minutes. Neither of them are able to hold this position. "We gotta head for the river."

"I know! I know!" shouts Nathaniels. "But we can't leave them behind."

Myers looks down at the two fallen comrades, Rathbone and Doggett, at his feet. Doggett has been shot in the right thigh and is in pain. Rathbone appears to have been temporarily blinded moments earlier; he's in shock.

"We can't just leave them to die in this field. I promised their mothers I would get them home," screams Myers.

He looks around. His face is dripping with blood from an unknown source—is he wounded too?—he is unable to see or think clearly. Adrenalin is the only thing keeping him, and his brothers in arms, alive.

As Myers adjusts his cap, ground fire whizzes past his ears; crackles and whistles; explosions and bangs. Enemy soldiers are in hot pursuit behind. Myers can hear their commands through the tall grass. It's now or never.

"You take Rathbone. I'll take Doggett. Follow me!"

Myers throws down his rifle and ammo bag—it's useless now—picks up Doggett, flings him over his shoulder and begins to move steadily eastwards. Nathaniels guides Rathbone by voice; he follows closely.

After a quarter of a mile—although it feels like 10 miles—the group emerges into plain sight, no cover, at the banks of the river. At the river's edge are scores of submerged, sunk or damaged canoes and vessels.

"Found one!" shouts Nathaniels to Myers, as he places a delirious Doggett on the ground. "This should make it."

The canoe is their only way to safety. They have mere minutes before the enemy catch up. If they do, they'll be hung up by their bootlaces by dinner.

Myers surveys the craft; it's small. "The canoe can only carry 100kg, maximum, at a time. Not enough for us all in one trip. How do we do this?" quizzes Nathaniels, testing the floating limits of the canoe with his foot. It's solid.

Myers looks at his squad and tries his best to calculate… but he was never very good with numbers. "OK, I weigh 80. Nathaniels?"

"I weigh 70," says Nathaniels. "And those two weigh 50 each, I reckon, the war's not been kind to them."

"And don't forget our medical bag—that's 10—we'll need that on the other side!" yells Doggett, clinging to the bag for dear life.

Gunpowder explodes in the near distance.

The enemy are closing in. The loudness of the gunfire increases behind the four tired and battle-beat men.

Myers is unable to think. It's all too much. He looks at Nathaniels. Both their eyes scream for help.

"I can't save us… I'm sorry," says Myers as tears stream from his eyes.

Just then, Rathbone speaks up for the first time.

"I can… but we must be quick."

How does Rathbone get his companions across the river safely?

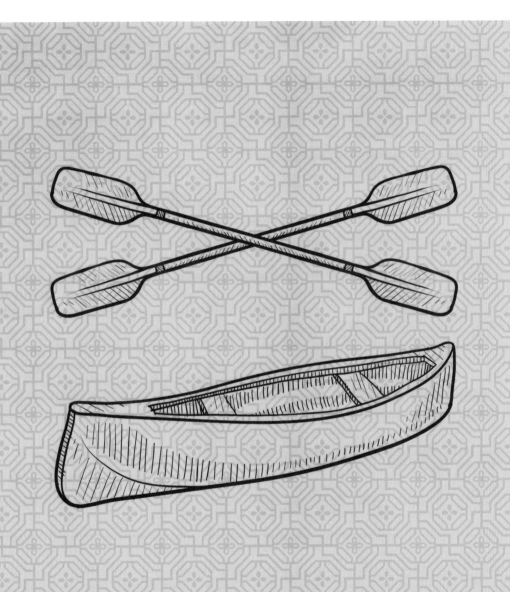

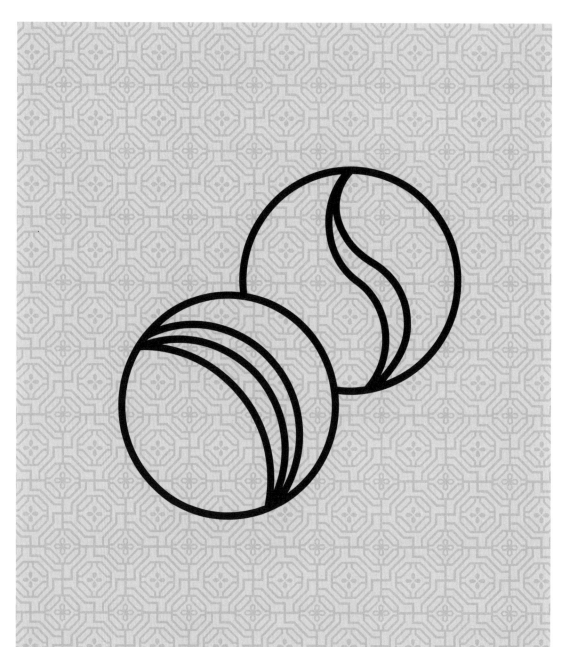

Lost Marbles

"He who is destined to defeat first fights,
and afterwards looks for victory."

Las Vegas, September 2023.

Heavyweight title bout between two bitter rivals. Whoever wins takes home the belt and becomes undisputed heavyweight champion. Whoever loses, loses.

In the red corner, there's the snarling American pit bull, Tyler James, weighing in at 250 pounds (113kg).

In the blue corner, there's the roaring British lion, Jimmy Jones, weighing in at 250 pounds (113kg).

In the fourth round, James delivers a stunning right-hand uppercut to Jones's jaw. It sends him to the floor. The referee counts to six before Jones gets up. The lion staggers around the cage, lost. Thankfully, he is saved by the bell—the round ends.

In the blue corner, Jones's coach is concerned that his boy has had his marbles knocked out of him. To check, the coach gives Jimmy a riddle:

"Look at me, Jimmy," says the coach. "I'm holding a bag filled with 27 marbles of three different hues: red, blue and green. The number of blue marbles is twice the number of red marbles, and the number of green marbles is three times the number of blue marbles. How many marbles of each shade are in the bag, Jimmy?"

Jones, in a daze, struggles to find his marbles.

But as the bell rings, Jones whispers the number to his coach. The fight continues…

How many marbles of each shade are in the bag?

A Light Issue

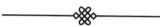

*"In war, then, let your great object be victory,
not lengthy campaigns."*

The labels have fallen off the light switch to the computer server room at DonTec. Tom, the IT guy, needs to know which switch operates it from a choice of three switches on the wall. Tom doesn't have time to get someone, put them in the room and turn the switches on one by one. Nor to go back and forth three times just in case. Plus, he likes a challenge and admires the logic problem this little conundrum presents. How can Tom figure out—in one try—which switch is the one to the light in the server room?

Pocketful of...

"The difficulty of tactical maneuvering consists in turning the devious into the direct, and misfortune into gain."

Talking in the boardroom one day, Hal comes up with a puzzle to try and fool his colleagues, none of whom think much of him. He comes up with the following: "My pocket is empty," he says, "but it still has something in it."

"Don't be dumb," says Filo.

"That's ridiculous," snorts Zoot, and his question is greeted with general disdain. However, once he reveals the answer, it turns out that he is not crazy, or stupid, but correct, and his colleagues develop a newfound respect for him. How?

Clowning Around

"Simulated fear postulates courage."

Jake has had a workplace rivalry with Rozza for years. Rozza is always mocking Jake's soccer team. Fed up with the taunts, Jake finally decides to get back at him. One day before a big match Jake says, "I'll bet you that I can predict the exact score of the game before it starts. The exact score." "No way—I'll take that bet," says Rozza. "OK, if you lose, and I correctly predict the score of the match before it starts, you have to come to work in a clown costume the Monday afterwards." "Sure thing," says Rozza, so sure of himself. However, the following Monday, there he is in a clown costume. How did Jake know the score?

An Arrangement

*"He will win who, prepared himself,
waits to take the enemy unprepared."*

"I've won!" shouts Sam, staring down at the lottery ticket.

"Let me check!" yells Sam's wife, Anita, thinking Sam is joking. She grabs the ticket from Sam's hand and looks carefully at each number.

8 – 5 – 49 – 17 – 6 – 3 and bonus ball 20.

"Oh my!" Anita says. "We've won!"

"That's what I meant," says Sam. "We've won!"

Anita looks down at the ticket and then back at the numbers on the TV.

"I don't recognize these numbers, though," Anita says. "I thought you played the family's birthdays. Whose birthdays are these?"

"No one's," says Sam. "I decided to play a particular set of numbers this week."

"Huh?!" exclaims Anita. "What's so special about these?"

Sam snatches back the ticket and rolls his eyes. "They're lucky!"

Besides being Sam's winning numbers, what else is significant about them?

Password

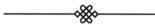

*"In battle, there are not more than two methods of attack—
the direct and the indirect; yet these two in combination
give rise to an endless series of maneuvers."*

Frank Metcalfe, a BioLabs assistant at a top-secret classified facility in ████████ one of the UK's advanced sites in pathogen and virus research, was desperate to get an immediate meeting with Prime Minister Denwood. He had vital data to share urgently. The state of the nation depended on it. All requests for access had been denied.

Metcalfe, tenacious and smart to a fault, took matters into his own hands. He drove down from his facility to a particular Westminster building, where he knew the PM would be that afternoon discussing electoral strategy for the upcoming election.

After locating the PM's whereabouts using a string of charm, cunning, manipulation and downright lies, Metcalfe stood within reach of the room where the PM resided.

Metcalfe, a hot and sweaty and unstable-looking mess, decided to gather his thoughts, tidy his report files, straighten his tie and generally compose himself before rushing toward the room unprepared.

Just then, Metcalfe observed that the room had a security agent standing guard outside the door. He also noticed that people were only entering the PM's room after telling the agent a word, or name, in reply to a name, or word, the agent gave them. It must be some kind of access code or password, Metcalfe thought. But it didn't make any sense. It all seemed so random.

Metcalfe, just out of sight of the agent, tuned into the passers-by as they attempted to enter the room to see if he could figure out the pattern. He didn't have time to waste. And he only had one shot to give the PM the news no leader of a nation wants to hear.

He listened closely:

Agent: "Fireplace"
Person 1: "David"
Agent: "Janitor"
Person 2: "Horatio"
Agent: "Unicorn"
Person 3: "Susie"
Agent: "Newspaper"
Person 4: "Lewis"
Agent: "Nuclear"
Person 5: "Lena"

What is the pattern?

Page 10
HEAVEN OR HEL

Bodil should ask of either guard: "What would the other guard say if I asked the way to Valhalla?" The answer from either will be the way to Hel, so he should take the opposite. The truth-teller will direct him to Hel, knowing that the other gatekeeper will lie. The liar will also point the way to Hel, because he's lying.

Page 12
THE JESTER'S RIDDLE

From the riddle, we can figure out that Mordred isn't telling the truth; if he were, there would be two knights. So Mordred is either the knave or the spy. Gareth also can't be the knight, because then his statement would be a lie. So that must mean that Lucan is the knight. Mordred, therefore, must be the spy, since the spy sometimes tells the truth; and that means Gareth is the knave.

Page 15
SHIELDS

Nechtan is the man who distributes weapons to the tribe's warriors.

Page 16
THE ROAD TO RUNE

ᚦᛟᚱᛁᛤ ᚲᛁ ᛟ ᛁᛏ ᛋᚺ ᚼ ᛗ ᛗ ᛗ ᚱ ᛏ ᛁ ᛗ ᛗ

= THOR IS KING. IT'S HAMMER TIME.

Page 18
A QUESTION OF ORDER

Cael, Aengus, Balor, Diarmaid, Elouan.

Page 19
ODIN'S WHISPER

BERSERKER. It is spelled out letter by letter at the start of each new sentence. Berserkers were famously rage-filled warriors in Norse lore.

Page 20
PLANT ME A KINGDOM

All the seeds were bad and wouldn't grow, but the girl was the only one honest enough to show this.

Page 23
THE WICKED WOODS

With one small step into the forest, you are no longer walking into it—you're walking through it. When it comes to conquering fear, the importance of that first step forward—and not backward—is all that matters.

Page 24
HALF A SHEEP

By placing two sheep on each corner, the shepherd could see four sheep out of each window.

Page 27
NEGOTIATIONS

The Grand Commandant had managed to increase production and training to *more* than 100 *shuang-shou* per month.

Page 28
ORDERS!

The commander's voice.

Page 30
HATS OFF TO YOU

Biluda, who can see that Dagrim has a white hat, realizes that their own hat must be a different shade from Dagrim's, because if it were the same, Adamen—who can see both—would have said something. Knowing their hat is a different hue from Dagrim's means that Biluda knows their own hat must be black.

Page 31
WARRIOR COUNT

Three—all except two had lost fingers, so one had lost fingers, one used a spear and one had lost an eye. The same is true for the other traits.

Page 33
CHOICES

The third door, because if the lion hasn't eaten for a month, it will be dead!

Page 34
DIADEMA

Aurum means gold in Latin. Gold is represented by "Au" on the periodic table. Crassus dies, famously, by having gold poured down his throat—a symbolic death reflective of his immense wealth.

Page 37
TRANSFORMATION

Iron ore.

Page 38
RIDDLE ME THIS

The letter V.

Page 40
CLEOPATRA'S DILEMMA

C	I	R	C	L	E
I	B	E	R	I	A
R	E	M	I	N	T
C	R	I	N	G	E
L	I	N	G	E	R
E	A	T	E	R	S

Page 42
MAKING MORE...

21. It is the Fibonacci sequence; each number is added to the previous one to make the next.

Page 43
TRIANGULATION

Two, as shown in the diagram.

Page 44
COST OF LIVING

The final square should have 40 in it. The first two rows are multiplied and then the first number is subtracted to give the result in the third column.

Page 46
WISHES

He wished to lose one hand (it's better than dying!).

Page 47
THERE WILL BE BLOOD
Quintus Valerii. In the Roman alphabet, Q is the 17th letter, or XVII. In the Roman alphabet, V is the 22nd letter, or XXII. There are only 23 letters in the Roman alphabet—no J, U or W.

Page 48
TIME TO THINK
Al-Mansur commanded the soldiers to start both hourglasses at the same time. Then, after the seven-minute hourglass ran out, to turn it over and start it again. Four minutes later, when the 11-minute hourglass ran out, to turn the seven-minute hourglass again. Then, to wait for the seven-minute hourglass to run out, which would take another four minutes. That's precisely 15 minutes.

Page 51
CENTURIONS
The winning order: Belenus, Decimus, Aelius, Cassisus, Egnatius.

Page 52
BROTHERS IN ARMS
The first letters of the Syrian city names spell KEEP THE BAG, a cruel joke from big brother al-Rashid regarding their "battle of the baggage" and the gift he sent.

Page 54
LEOFRIC AND GODIVA
The law is simple: access via double-lettered words—toll, door, hurry, battle. The man would be allowed to enter with almost any double-letter word.

Page 56
A CAGED LION

The foods Richard received from the guard spelled out a clue: KEY UNDER STONE.

K - Karotte (carrot)

E - Erbse (pea)

Y - Ysop (hyssop, a culinary herb)

U - Urdbohne (lentil)

N - Nuss (nut)

D - Dill (dill, an herb)

E - Endivie (endive, a leafy green)

R - Radieschen (radish)

S - Salbei (sage, a herb)

T - Thymian (thyme, a herb)

O - Olive (olive)

N - Nelke (clove, a spice)

E - Eiche (oak leaf, used in traditional dishes)

Page 58
GOLDEN RATIO

Using only addition, subtraction, multiplication and division, the solution is:

$888 + 88 + 8 + 8 + 8 = 1,000$

Page 61
JEST A MINUTE

The letter E.

Page 62
DEDUCTION

No, because if it were true, that would mean one of the Merry Men would be telling the truth. One must be a knight, and the other one of the Merry Men.

Page 65
WHAT DO YOU SEE?

Your shadow.

Page 66
LOGISTICS

First he took Jérôme and the cheese across, and came back with only the dog, leaving it on the shore. Then he carried the chicken across, and came back with the cheese. Finally he took the dog and the cheese across, and was only then able to continue his journey home… to a good meal.

Page 68
THE CELLAR DOOR

+5 -2 is the sequence so 1 + 5, give the second digit 6. 6 - 2, gives the third digit 4. This makes the next two entries in the series 12, and 10. Of course, in real life Guy Fawkes was highly intelligent, so he would have figured out the code in seconds and gone on to light up the night—if only those guards hadn't come to arrest him!

Page 70
CHEERS!

Four—the number of cheers matches the number of letters in the word.

Page 71
HUNTING TIME

Noon.

Page 72
REARRANGING THE LINES

Start

1

2

3

Finish

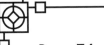

Page 74
FINAL WORDS

N.P. LATECOMER is an anagram of MERTON PLACE, Nelson's famous Surrey home, and where his great love, Emma Hamilton, famously resided to mourn the loss of Horatio with Nelson's daughter, Horatia. Despite being one of the great ocean explorers, Nelson sincerely adored his home at Merton Place. Nelson was famed for his innovative strategic thinking and tactics; "Nelson's Touch"—two columns of attack perpendicular to each other—became the strategy of legend.

Page 76
A GLASS HALF FULL

Alexander intends to poison the river below his camp, but upstream of the enemy camp with the excess gunpowder, polluting their water source. Gunpowder, when consumed in water, leads to intestinal issues that would slow the large army's progress considerably.

Page 79
LETTERS FROM ABROAD

The body of the letter is 84 words long. John no longer counts the days, so 84 divided by 12 months = 7 years. It is the Seven Years' War (1756–1763)—the "Empire" clue should help.

Page 80
FINDERS KEEPERS

Cable's best strategy to maximize his chances of winning is to choose heads every time, or tails every time. If he chooses heads, there are two possible good outcomes: (heads, tails) and (tails, heads). They both result in a win for Cable.

If Cable chooses tails every time, there are also two possible good outcomes: (tails, heads) and (heads, tails). However, these are the same two outcomes as when he chooses heads, so are identical. Since the outcomes are the same regardless of his

choice, it's better to stick with one consistent choice—unlike Cable and Swigert's attitude to fighting.

Page 83
LIGHT IN THE NIGHT
The match.

Page 84
WASTING TIME
Mississippi.

Page 86
FRENEMIES
Forty is the only number in English spelled with its letters in alphabetical order.

Page 89
A BURNING QUESTION
They light one end of one fuse, and both ends of the other. When the double-ended fuse has burned through, exactly 30 minutes will have passed. Then they light the other end of the first fuse. When that has burned through, exactly 15 minutes will have passed: the cannons will fire on time!

Page 90
MEXICAN STANDOFF
It is nearly impossible to ride a bicycle through dense sand. Petey dumped the bike and ran away to live another day. Paulie fared better on the unicycle, but by the time he arrived at the munitions store, Pokey shot him. Pokey arrived first on foot and had enough time to reload his gun. He shot Paulie.

Page 92
OLD ENEMIES

Seven. It's the most probable outcome in a roll of two dice. You're six times more likely to roll a 7 than a 2 or a 12, a significant difference. You're twice as likely to roll a 7 than a 4 or a 10. However, it's only 1.2 times more likely you will roll a 7 than a 6 or an 8. Barrio also uses language to steer López away from thinking of the number 7.

Page 94
RESISTANCE

A guerrilla. The term originates from the Spanish word *guerrilla,* which means "little war" or "warrior." The riddle comprises a particular set of tactics that are used when discussing guerrilla warfare. The term gained prominence during the Peninsular War (1808–1814) in Spain. Spanish irregular fighters, known as *guerrilleros,* resisted the French occupation led by Napoleon Bonaparte's forces. The guerrilleros engaged in non-conventional warfare tactics against the better-equipped French troops.

Page 96
WAR HERO

It is the date of birth of his second child, Lucia. Lucia was the best birthday gift as he was born on the General's 30th birthday, which was the same year the safe was installed, inspiring him to set the code using the date, 03-19-31. However, as per the General's caveat that it takes him 'back in time' it should be entered in reverse, 31-19-03.

Page 100
LEADERSHIP

The number zero.

Page 102
DIVIDE AND CONQUER

Bernadotte's *chasse au trésor,* or scavenger hunt, spells Austerlitz. The Battle of Austerlitz (1805) was widely regarded as one of Napoleon's greatest victories; he decisively defeated the combined forces of Russia and Austria, leading to the Treaty of Pressburg and further consolidating French power in Europe.

1. A = antique clock
2. U = umbrella
3. S = silverware
4. T = teapot
5. E = *escritoire* (a small writing desk)
6. R = rug
7. L = lantern
8. I = inkwell
9. T = trunk
10. Z – zither, a stringed instrument

Page 105
A LUCKY FIND

The crate!

Page 106
ANGELS AND DEMONS

31	73	7
13	37	61
67	1	43

All the numbers are odd, and prime too—except for the 1, obviously.

Page 109
FOOL A FOOL

Yesterday, today and tomorrow.

Page 110
BEHIND ENEMY LINES

General Darcy poisoned Commander Aldridge with a toxin hidden in the wine. Darcy, standing behind Aldridge, was the only general who didn't act when Aldridge fell down. Darcy's "ice-cold" determination also "froze" at the moment Aldridge fell, because he knew what was happening.

Page 113
ON THE RUN

One—Sergei is the only one fleeing!

Page 115
HORSEPLAY

He suggested they switch horses, then the winner (still the owner of the slower horse) wins the race in more ways than one.

MASTERPIECES

The jar tagged green cannot contain green paint (hint 2), so it must contain either blue or red paint. However, since the jar tagged blue contains yellow paint (hint 3), the jar tagged green must contain red paint.

The jar tagged red contains green paint (hint 2).

The jar tagged blue contains yellow paint (hint 3).

Since the jar tagged green contains red paint, and the jar tagged red contains green paint, we have deduced that the shades in these two jars are switched. This means that the actual shades are:

Jar tagged green: red paint

Jar tagged red: green paint

Jar tagged blue: yellow paint

Based on the deductions, the remaining shades are blue and purple. So, the actual shades in the remaining jars are:

Jar tagged yellow: blue paint

Jar tagged purple: purple paint

The correct arrangement of the actual paint shades in the jars is:

Jar tagged green: red paint

Jar tagged red: green paint

Jar tagged blue: yellow paint

Jar tagged yellow: blue paint

Jar tagged purple: purple paint

Page 118
WHITE HOUSE DOWN

The missing number in the sequence is 63.

In the sequence 1, 3, 7, 15, 31, ?, 127, the pattern is that each number is multiplied by 2 and then increased by 1.

1 x 2 + 1 = 3

3 x 2 + 1 = 7

7 x 2 + 1 = 15

15 x 2 + 1 = 31

31 x 2 + 1 = 63 (missing number)

63 x 2 + 1 = 127

Page 120
WINDS OF TIME

Tomorrow.

Page 122
RENEGADES

The answer to the question is: none. There are no words here—we told you—it's pure anarchy!

Page 124
TIRED TALK

Footsteps.

Page 125
PAYOUT

The crafty soldiers should take one gold piece from the first bag, two pieces from the second, three from the third bag, and so on, until the fifth bag, and put that combined weight on the scales. If the weight on the scale ends in .1, they will know that the first bag contains the fake precious metal. If the scale weight ends in .2, then it must be the second bag that contains the fake gold, and so on.

Page 126
LOAD THE WAGONS

Private Shaw should load all the carts with ammunition. That way he has done what was requested, loaded half with ammo—and the other half too.

Page 128
BATTLE OF EQUALS

A game of chess.

Page 129
SHOOTIN' TALK

Into the ground! Mr Feo will shoot at Mr Malo first, and if Mr Malo survives, he will shoot at Mr Feo first.

Page 131
SUPPLIES

Open the box labelled Mixed Fruit. If it contains apples, you know that it's the apples crate, for all have incorrect labels. Likewise, the crate labelled Apples must contain bananas, and the crate marked Bananas must contain the mixture.

Page 132
THE BRIDGE

Clockwise.

Page 133
CAPTURE!

The same amount—six. One hour is 10 times as long as six minutes, so that's the time needed to catch 10 times as many prisoners.

Page 134
GIVE AND TAKE

Nowhere! This one is all in the presentation of information. There are 25 groats in the innkeeper's bag, two in his pocket and one in each of the mercenary's pockets—that makes 30!

Page 135
BRIDGE OVER TROUBLED WATER

21 minutes, as follows:

Jacquouille and Godefroy cross first (3 mins)

Jacquouille returns with the torch (5 mins)

Frénégonde and Édouard cross (15 mins)

Godefroy returns with the torch (18 mins)

Godefroy and Jacquouille cross together (21 mins)

Page 136
CODED MESSAGE

He orders the attack—the first letters of each word in the message spell out ATTACK NOW.

Page 138
LONG DIVISION

The numbers in the left column start at 7 and go down by 1 each time. The missing number on the right is 5, the sum of the numbers in the first two columns.

Page 141
ADDING UP

100. It is the next number that does not contain a T when spelled out.

Page 142
AN ODD NUMBER

Auf Wiedersehen, or goodbye. "Auf Wiedersehen" is how Einstein famously said goodbye—in German. Einstein retired from Princeton University on December 18, 1945, a clue given at the start of the puzzle; 151 is also a whole number, but an odd one. Just like Einstein.

151 is the total letter-to-number conversion of the words "auf Wiedersehen."

$$A + U + F + W + I + E + D + E + R + S + E + H + E + N =$$

$$1 + 21 + 6 + 23 + 9 + 5 + 4 + 5 + 18 + 19 + 5 + 8 + 5 + 14 = 151$$

Page 145
DECISION TIME

The number of battalions equals the number of vowels in the number, so Six will have one.

Page 146
EXTRACTION

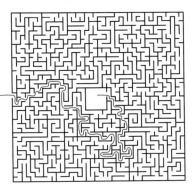

Page 148
DEATH BY...?

Gerald was doing a parachute jump and his parachute (the package) had failed to open. He landed on the island.

Page 150
SELF-DESTRUCT

Page 153
WARNING

There were three men in the forest: a man, his son and his grandson.

Page 154
PLANS

To figure out Ben's identity, he should ask them all, "Are you Charles?" Archie will reply no, because he's telling the truth. Ben will reply yes, because he's a liar, but Charles will say no, because he's lying.

Page 157
CROSSY ROAD

It was a bright, sunny day!

Page 158
PSYCHOLOGICAL WARFARE

1, 14, 1, 18, 13, 25, 13, 1, 18, 3, 8, 5, 19, 15, 14, 9, 20, 19, 19, 20, 15, 13, 1, 3, 8, when converted from numbers to letters (A = 1, etc.) = "An army marches in its stomach," Napoleon's famous quote about military strategy.

Page 161
AGENT OF CHAOS

Big Ben, London, 2.50pm.

Page 163
BOARDROOM BRAVADO

"Your precise weight."

Page 164
INFINITE ALTERNATE

The obituary contains seemingly random punctuation errors that, when compiled together, in order, via the given key, spell: I AM NOTHING WITHOUT YOU, or

$$(\; ! = + \{ : * (+ \& , (: * \{ \text{“} : / \{ \text{“}$$

Bridge's acknowledgment let Miles know that their rivalry pushed him to greatness. And vice versa.

Page 169
KNOCK KNOCK

You wouldn't knock on the door of your own room!

Page 170
HOPE SPRINGS

Dusty had seen just a mirage, that's all. The starting letter of each sentence spells MIRAGE.

Page 173
SQUABBLING SIBLINGS

Jackson places the piece of paper under a doorway with the door shut with one child on each side.

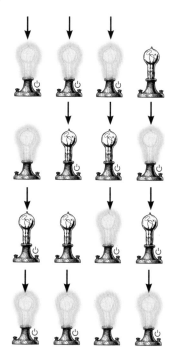

Page 174
HEADS OR TAILS

Four moves. The diagram shows which ones to make.

Page 177
PULL THE PIN

I am a number between 3,000 and 4,000—the first digit must be 3.

My first digit is one-third of my second digit—Since the first digit is 3, the second digit must be 9 (3 x 3 = 9).

My third digit starts the sum of my first and second digits—the sum of the first and second digits (3 + 9) is 12, so the third digit is 1.

My fourth digit is twice my third digit—twice the third digit (1 x 2) is 2, so the fourth digit is 2.

The correct four-digit combination is 3912.

Page 178
CATCH AND RELEASE

D L Y 8 0 R E backwards is E R 0 8 Y L D. And shifted three places backwards in a letter-number conversion—a clue given twice—makes B O L I V I A, Morales's nationality, with the binary numbers 0 and 1 switched around.

Page 181
MUST. DO. IT.

An itch.

Page 182
DRINK UP!

Coffee. Two Es in the name drink coffee, one E drinks water, no Es drink tea.

Page 185
THE ENIGMA

The sign reads: "Behind this door kingdom come awaits. Unless you noticed the trip wire." Arnett has fallen back so that they may assess the scene and find the trip wire. The sign is written using a Caesar Cipher. Each letter has been shifted three positions forward in the alphabet.

Page 186
ALL-SEEING EYE

A traffic light.

Page 189
NEW BLOOD

The answer is *no*, you can't solve this. Reynolds wants someone who works for him to be brave enough to tell him the right answer, which is no.

Page 192
DETONATION SEQUENCE

The sequence is an 11-rung word ladder, as invented by Lewis Carroll.

The missing rungs are:

DATA
DATE
SATE
SITE
SITS
SETS
SEES
SEEP
STEP
STOP
ATOP
ATOM

Page 195
BRAVO THREE ECHO

Three assailants. Two assailants are in front of the last assailant; the first assailant has two assailants behind; one assailant is between the other two.

Page 197
NUMERICAL ADVANTAGE

The square of the previous number, plus one ($2^2 + 1 = 5$; $5^2 + 1 = 26$, etc.)

The next number is 458,330.

Page 198
WARGAMES

If we look at the price of Medic Pack & 60-Second Shield, we can see that both of them are priced at $1. Because they must be priced at least $1, and since they cost $2 together, they must cost $1 separately. We can now solve the rest.

For instance:

Glock 26 & Medic Pack = $5

Now, we know the Medic Pack costs $1

Thus, Glock 26 + $1 = $5

Glock 26 = $4

You can find out the price for each one of the weapons in a similar fashion. So, 60-Second Shield = $1; Medic Pack = $1; Hand Grenade = $3; Silencer = $2; Glock 26= $4; Rocket Launcher = $2; Flamethrower = $3; AK47 = $4

Page 201
EXPENDING ENERGY

Running out of petrol (gasoline).

Page 202
ON MY MIND

A lawsuit.

Page 205
GIVING AND RECEIVING

Two—he gives half away each time, but receives another one in return.

Page 206
WHEN THE WIND BLOWS
Using a burning log, he sets fire to the wood behind him. The wind carries the flame, burning out in time for him to walk through the ashes to safety.

Page 208
SIMPLE SEQUENCE
13112221—the pattern describes the numbers in the previous line, as spoken: "one," "one one," "one two and one one," etc.

Page 209
HELD HOSTAGE
The letter U.

Page 210
FLIGHT NOT FIGHT
They took off on different days.

Page 211
SHORT CUT TO SUCCESS
The one with the messy hair, because he must cut the (neat) hair of the other one!

Page 212
THE ELITE SQUAD

The roles should be reassigned as such:

Sniper: Medic

Demolition: Recon

Reconnaissance: Sniper

Medic: Demolition

Page 215
ACROSS THE RIVER

Rathbone rows the injured Doggett across, guided by Doggett's navigation. Rathbone returns, guided by Myers's voice. Myers then rows over, and Doggett returns. Doggett and Rathbone row across again, Doggett returns. Nathaniels rows across with the medicine bag, and Doggett returns. Doggett and Rathbone row across again for the last time.

Page 219
LOST MARBLES

There are 3 red marbles, 6 blue marbles, and 18 green marbles in the bag.

Page 220
A LIGHT ISSUE

He turns on switch one for five minutes, then turns it off and activates switch two. He opens the door—if the light is on, it's switch two. If it's off but the bulb is cold, it's switch three. If it's off but the light is warm, it's switch one.

Page 221
POCKETFUL OF...

He has a hole in his pocket.

Page 222
CLOWNING AROUND

He didn't, but as the match started, he predicted the score would be 0–0. Any match has no score "before it starts"!

Page 225
AN ARRANGEMENT

The first letters of the numbers run in alphabetical order:

8 (e) – 5 (f) – 4 (f) 9 (n) – 1 (o) 7 (s) – 6 (s) – 3 (t) with the bonus ball 2 (t) 0 (z)

Page 226
PASSWORD

The agent speaks a random word. The answer must be a name that begins two letters earlier in the alphabet and contains at least two of the same letters.